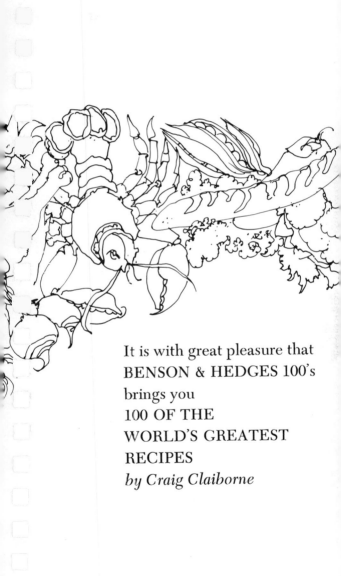

It is with great pleasure that
BENSON & HEDGES 100's
brings you
100 OF THE
WORLD'S GREATEST
RECIPES
*by Craig Claiborne*

All photographs are by Bill Aller, Gene Maggio and Al Wegner of The New York Times Studio with the exception of the following: page 130, Robert McCabe; page 84 and page 126, Bradley Olman; page 128 courtesy of Seagram's.

Acknowledgment is gratefully extended to Mollie E. C. Webster for her assistance in preparation of the manuscript and also to Miss Ann Bramson.

Permission to reprint from the following sources is gratefully acknowledged:

*Craig Claiborne's Favorites from The New York Times,* Quadrangle/The New York Times Book Co.

*The Craig Claiborne Journal,* Claiborne-Franey Inc.

*The New York Times International Cookbook,* Harper & Row, Publishers, Inc.

*The New York Times Cookbook,* Harper & Row, Publishers, Inc.

Published by
Philip Morris Incorporated
for Benson & Hedges 100's
100 Park Avenue
New York, New York 10017

Printed in the United States of America.

## FOREWORD

For the past twenty years, it has been both my pleasure and occupation to travel the world in pursuit of recipes. I have been privileged to enjoy many an unforgettable meal. The opportunities to interview renowned chefs throughout the world have been a constant source of delight. Many have made this country their home and have adapted their native dishes to the ingredients available here.

I am frequently asked which particular cuisine would be my choice, if I were restricted to only one.

I am deeply attached to the foods of China and India. Yet I often find myself thinking aloud of the Haitian rice and black mushroom dish you will find on page 45. It is hard to envision permanently foregoing the fish soup on page 36. I have lingered long over spinach pies on a Greek Isle (page 4), savored the last morsel of Danish gravlax (page 1), and fondly recall the wonderful nuoc mam sauce of Vietnam that you'll find on page 63.

And, after several weeks in these faraway places, I realize that a craving for American corned beef can be profound.

In short, I have no one favorite cuisine. Rather, I revel in a long list of favorite recipes from many cuisines.

The 100 recipes you will find here are adapted to the American kitchen without losing their characteristic charm and gratification. If they give you even a portion of the satisfaction they've given me, I guarantee you'll be pleased.

## CONTENTS

*Scandinavia*

## Gravlax

*(Salt- and sugar-cured salmon)*

*Yield: 12 to 20 servings*

2   bunches fresh dill
1   3½—4-pound section of fresh salmon,
    preferably cut from the center of the fish
¼   cup kosher salt
¼   cup sugar
1   teaspoon coarsely ground white pepper
    Mustard-dill sauce (see recipe, page 6)

1. Cut off and discard any very tough stems from the dill. Rinse the dill and pat it dry.

2. Bone the salmon section or have it boned. There should be 2 fillets of equal size and weight. Do not rinse the fish but pat it dry with paper toweling.

3. Combine the salt, sugar, and pepper. Rub this mixture into the pink flesh of the salmon.

4. Spread ⅓ of the dill over the bottom of a flat dish. Add one of the salmon pieces, skin side down. Cover this with another ⅓ of the dill. Add the remaining piece of salmon, placing it sandwich-fashion over the dill, skin side up. Cover with the remaining dill and place a plate on top. Add a sizable weight and let it stand in a very cool place or in the refrigerator for 48 hours. Turn the "sandwich" every 12 hours, always covering with the plate and weighting it down. Serve thinly sliced on the bias, like smoked salmon, with mustard-dill sauce.

## **Chicken Chat**
*(A salad/appetizer)*

*Yield: 4 to 6 servings*

| | |
|---|---|
| 1 | large chicken breast, about ¾ pound |
| 3 | cups fresh or canned chicken broth, approximately |
| ½ | cup chopped mint leaves |
| ½ | cup chopped fresh coriander leaves (see note) |
| 2 | mild or hot long green chilies |
| ½ | cup plus ⅓ cup chopped onion |
| ½ | cup chopped tomato |
| 1 | teaspoon grated fresh ginger |
| ¼ | teaspoon ground coriander seeds |
| 1 | teaspoon finely chopped garlic |
| | Salt and freshly ground black pepper to taste |
| ⅛ | teaspoon cayenne or more to taste |
| 3 | tablespoons lemon juice or more to taste |
| 2 | tablespoons yogurt |
| 2 | tablespoons grenadine syrup |
| ½ | cup seeded diced tomato |
| ⅓ | cup finely diced seeded cucumber |
| 1 | very sweet seedless navel orange, optional |
| ½ | banana, optional |
| | Lettuce leaves |
| | Coriander leaves for garnish |

1. Place the chicken breast in a saucepan and add chicken broth to cover. Bring to the boil. Partially cover and simmer 15 minutes. Turn off the heat and let stand until cool.

2. Combine the chopped mint and coriander leaves in the container of an electric blender. Split the chilies in half and chop coarsely. Add them to the blender. Add ½ cup chopped onion, chopped tomato, ginger, ground coriander seeds, garlic, salt, pepper, cayenne, lemon juice, yogurt, and grenadine syrup. Blend thoroughly.

3. Skin and bone the chicken breast. Pull the meat into sizable bite-size pieces. Refrigerate chicken broth for other use. Place the chicken pieces in a mixing bowl. Add the diced tomato, remaining ⅓ cup chopped onion, and cucumber. If the orange and banana are used, peel

them and cut into small cubes. Add them to the chicken. Add the blender sauce and toss well. Refrigerate until ready to use. Serve on a bed of lettuce leaves and garnish with coriander leaves.

Note: Fresh coriander leaves, which are also known as cilantro and culantro in Spanish, are available in Chinese, Spanish, Mexican, and Indian markets.

*Italy*

## Carpaccio
*(Sliced raw beef)*

*Yield: 6 servings*

| | |
|---|---|
| 1¼ | pounds raw lean beef, preferably top round |
| ½ | cup white vinegar |
| 12 | very small sour pickles, preferably imported French cornichons |
| ½ | cup finely chopped parsley |
| 2 | cloves garlic, finely minced |
| 3 | anchovy fillets |
| ½ | cup capers |
| 3 | tablespoons coarsely chopped onion |
| ⅓ | cup mustard, preferably imported mustard such as Dijon or Düsseldorf, or use domestic creole or spicy mustard (do not use ball-park mustard) |
| ¾ | cup olive oil |

1. Trim the meat carefully to remove all outside fat. Have the meat sliced as thinly as possible. (Cut across the grain.) If a good, sturdy electric slicer is not available, the meat may be partially frozen to facilitate slicing with a very sharp knife.

2. Arrange the meat neatly in 1 layer on 1 large or 2 medium-size serving dishes.

3. Put the remaining ingredients into the container of an electric blender or a food processor. Blend without overblending. The sauce should have a slight texture. Serve the sauce with the meat on the side to be dipped into it or spoon the sauce over the meat.

3

## **Spanakopitta**
*(Greek spinach pie)*

*Yield: 18 or more servings*

| | |
|---|---|
| 3 | pounds fresh spinach |
| ¾ | cup olive oil, approximately |
| 2 | bundles scallions, trimmed and chopped |
| ¼ | cup chopped parsley |
| ½ | pound feta cheese, crumbled |
| 6 | eggs, lightly beaten |
| | Salt and freshly ground black pepper |
| ½ | pound or 10 sheets phyllo pastry (see note) |

1. Preheat the oven to 350 degrees.

2. Pick over the spinach to remove and discard all blemished leaves and tough stems. Rinse the spinach in several changes of cold water to remove all traces of sand. Steam the spinach briefly over boiling water just until the leaves are wilted. Let cool. Chop the spinach coarsely.

3. Heat 1 tablespoon of oil in a skillet and add the scallions. Cook, stirring, until they are wilted.

4. In a mixing bowl, combine the spinach, scallions, parsley, cheese, eggs, salt and pepper to taste. Add 1 tablespoon of oil and blend thoroughly.

5. Select a baking pan measuring approximately 13 by 9 inches. Or use a round pan of similar size. Cover the pan with 1 layer of phyllo pastry, letting the edges of the pastry hang over the sides. Brush the pastry generously with oil. Continue adding 4 more layers, brushing each layer with oil as it is added. Spoon the spinach mixture into the center and smooth it over. Cover with another layer of phyllo, brush with oil and continue adding 4 more layers, brushing oil between each layer. Use a sharp knife or scissors to trim off the overhanging edges of pastry. Bake the pie for 40 to 50 minutes or until it is piping hot throughout and golden brown on top.

Note: Phyllo pastry is available in most food shops and stores specializing in Greek foods.

## Schun Lee Shrimp
*(Tangy Spicy Shrimp)*

*Yield: 6 to 8 servings*

- ½    pound raw shrimp
- 1    cup finely chopped scallions
- 1    clove garlic, finely minced
- 1    teaspoon finely chopped fresh hot green or red chili pepper
- 1    teaspoon finely chopped fresh ginger
- 1    teaspoon shao hsing or dry sherry
      Salt
- 1    teaspoon monosodium glutamate, optional
- ½    teaspoon freshly ground white pepper
- 1    teaspoon five spice powder (see note)
- 1    tablespoon or more chili paste with garlic (see note)
- 1    tablespoon hot oil (see note)
- 1½   teaspoons sesame oil

1. Shell and devein the shrimp. If the shrimp are large, cut them in half. Bring enough water to cover the shrimp to the boil. Add the shrimp and cook about 1 minute. Drain. Run under cold running water. Pat dry. Refrigerate.

2. Combine the remaining ingredients and pour over the shrimp. Serve cold.

Note: Bottled chili paste with garlic and bottled hot oil are widely available in Chinese groceries. Five spice powder is a blend of ground anise, fennel, cloves, cinnamon, and Szechuan peppercorns. It is available in Chinese groceries. Warning: These are very spicy shrimp.

*Scandinavia*

## Senapssos Räkor
*(Shrimp with Mustard-Dill Sauce)*

*Yield: 6 or more servings*

| | |
|---|---|
| 2 | pounds raw shrimp in the shell |
| 1 | bay leaf |
| 12 | whole allspice |
| 6 | sprigs parsley |
| 1 | rib celery with leaves, quartered |
| | Water |
| | Salt |
| 10 | peppercorns, crushed |
| 1¼ | cups mustard-dill sauce (see recipe) |

1. Combine the shrimp, bay leaf, allspice, parsley, celery, water, salt, and peppercorns in a saucepan.

2. Bring to the boil and turn off the heat. Let the shrimp cool in the cooking liquid. Drain and chill.

3. Shell and devein the shrimp and serve with the mustard-dill sauce.

## *Mustard-Dill Sauce*

*Yield: 1¼ cups*

| | |
|---|---|
| 1 | egg yolk |
| 1 | teaspoon wine vinegar |
| 3 | tablespoons prepared mustard, preferably Dijon or Düsseldorf |
| | A few drops of Tabasco |
| | Salt and freshly ground black pepper |
| 1 | cup oil, preferably a light olive oil, or a combination of olive oil and peanut, vegetable, or corn oil |
| | Lemon juice, optional |
| ¼ | cup finely chopped fresh dill |

1. Place the yolk in a mixing bowl and add the vinegar, 1 tablespoon mustard, Tabasco, salt and pepper to taste. Beat vigorously for a second or two with a wire whisk or electric beater.

2. Start adding the oil gradually, beating continuously with the whisk or electric beater. Continue beating and adding oil until all of it is used. Taste the sauce and add more salt to taste

and the lemon juice if desired. Beat in the remaining mustard and the dill. If all the sauce is not to be used immediately, beat in a tablespoon of water. This will help stabilize the sauce.

Note: The mustard-dill sauce can also be served with any kind of cold steamed shellfish or cold poached fish or hard-boiled eggs.

## **Chicken Soong**
*(Cubed chicken in lettuce leaves)*

*Yield: 6 to 12 servings*

| | |
|---|---|
| 1 | head iceberg lettuce |
| 1 | large, boned chicken breast, about 1 pound |
| 1 | egg white |
| ½ | teaspoon salt |
| 2 | tablespoons cornstarch |
| 2 | long green chilies, hot or mild |
| 10 | or 12 water chestnuts, canned or, preferably, fresh |
| ½ | cup finely diced celery |
| 3 | tablespoons finely diced carrots |
| 1 | teaspoon chopped fresh ginger |
| 2 | teaspoons or more finely chopped garlic |
| 3 | tablespoons finely chopped scallion |
| 2 | tablespoons shao hsing or dry sherry |
| ½ | tablespoon light soy sauce |
| ½ | tablespoon chili paste with garlic |
| 1 | teaspoon sugar |
| 1 | teaspoon monosodium glutamate, optional |
| 1 | tablespoon water |
| 2 | cups peanut, vegetable, or corn oil |
| ½ | teaspoon sesame oil |

1. Core the lettuce and separate it into leaves. Pile on a platter and set aside.

2. Place the chicken breast on a flat surface and, holding a sharp kitchen knife almost parallel to the cutting surface, cut the breast into the thinnest possible slices. Stack the slices and cut into shreds. Cut the shreds into tiny cubes. There should be about 2 cups.

3. Place the chicken meat in a mixing bowl and add the egg white, salt and 1 tablespoon cornstarch. Blend well with the fingers. Refrigerate 30 minutes or longer.

4. Core the chilies. Split them in half, seed and shred them. Cut the shreds into small cubes. There should be between ¼ and ½ cup.

5. Slice the water chestnuts thinly. Cut the slices into small cubes. There should be about ½ cup.

6. Combine the chopped chilies, water chest-

nuts, celery, carrots, and ginger. Set aside.

7. In another bowl, combine the garlic and scallion and set aside.

8. Combine the wine, soy sauce, chili paste with garlic, sugar, monosodium glutamate, and set aside.

9. Combine the remaining 1 tablespoon of cornstarch and the water and stir to blend. Set aside.

10. Heat the peanut oil in a wok or skillet and when it is hot, add the chicken, stirring constantly to separate the cubes. Cook about 1½ minutes and drain. Set aside.

11. Return 2 tablespoons of the oil to the wok and add the celery and water chestnut mixture. Cook, stirring, about 30 seconds and add the scallion and garlic. Cook, stirring, about 10 seconds and add the chicken. Cook, stirring, about 30 seconds or until the chicken is piping hot. Add the wine and soy sauce mixture and the sesame oil. Stir the cornstarch mixture until smooth and add it quickly. Stir rapidly about 30 seconds and transfer to a hot platter.

12. Serve the chicken with the lettuce on the side. Let each guest help himself, adding a spoonful or so of the chicken mixture to a lettuce leaf, folding it before eating.

*Peru*

## Ceviche with Scallops and Striped Bass

*(Pickled raw fish)*                    Yield: 6 servings

| | |
|---|---|
| 1 | pound bay scallops |
| ½ | pound boneless, skinless striped bass, cut into ¾-inch cubes |
| 1 | clove garlic, finely chopped |
| 2 | bay leaves, crumbled |
| 1 | teaspoon crushed red pepper flakes |
| ¾ | cup lime juice |
| 1 | lime, cut in fine dice |
| ⅓ | cup chopped scallions |

Combine all the ingredients and refrigerate. Serve with slices of French or Italian bread.

*Russia*

## Caviar

That most elegant of appetizers. Serve it ice cold on toast with butter, thinly sliced onion rings, finely chopped hard-boiled egg yolks and whites, and a dash of lemon juice.

*France*

## Coquilles St. Jacques aux Tomates et Paprika

*(Scallops with tomato and paprika sauce)*

*Yield: 6 servings*

| | |
|---|---|
| 1 | pound scallops |
| 4 | tablespoons butter |
| | Salt and freshly ground black pepper |
| ¼ | cup cognac |
| 1 | cup tomato sauce (see note) |
| 1 | teaspoon paprika |
| 1 | teaspoon finely chopped garlic |
| 3 | tablespoons finely chopped parsley |
| 6 | teaspoons grated Gruyère or Parmesan cheese |

1. Preheat the oven to 450 degrees.

2. If the scallops are very large, cut them into 3 or 4 crosswise slices. If they are medium, cut them in half. If they are very small, leave them whole.

3. Heat 2 tablespoons of butter and add the scallops and salt and pepper to taste. Cook, shaking the skillet, about 2 minutes. Add the cognac and ignite it. Cook about 1 minute and add the tomato sauce, paprika, garlic, parsley, salt, and pepper. Cook about 2 minutes.

4. Spoon equal amounts of the mixture into 6 scallop shells or individual ramekins. Sprinkle each with 1 teaspoon of cheese and 1 teaspoon of butter. Arrange on a baking dish and bake 10 minutes.

Note: To make a quick tomato sauce, cook 2 cups of peeled, chopped tomatoes, fresh or canned, until reduced to 1 cup. Add salt and pepper to taste.

## **Pâté Maison**

*Yield: 20 or more servings*

| | |
|---|---|
| 4 | tablespoons butter |
| ¼ | pound fresh mushrooms, rinsed well, patted dry, and finely chopped |
| ½ | cup finely chopped shallots (or use an equal quantity of finely chopped onion in addition to that listed below) |
| 1½ | cups finely chopped onions |
| 1½ | tablespoons finely chopped garlic |
| ½ | teaspoon dried thyme |
| 1 | bay leaf, chopped or ½ teaspoon powdered bay leaf |
| | Salt and freshly ground black pepper, a liberal amount |
| ¼ | pound ham sliced ¼-inch thick |
| ½ | cup cognac |
| 2 | pounds lean and fat boneless pork shoulder or loin (there should be about 2 parts fat to 1 part lean), ground |
| 1 | pound pork or calves liver, ground or blended |
| 2 | large or 3 small eggs |
| ½ | cup heavy cream |
| ¼ | teaspoon ground allspice |
| ⅛ | teaspoon grated nutmeg |
| ½ | teaspoon ground or chopped dried rosemary |
| ½ | pound chicken livers |
| ½ | cup shelled pistachios |

1. Heat the butter and add the chopped mushrooms, shallots, onions, garlic, thyme, and bay leaf. Add salt and pepper to taste and cook, stirring frequently, until the mushrooms give up their juices. Continue cooking and stirring until the mixture becomes "dry" without browning. Let cool.

2. Cut the ham slice into ¼-inch strips. Place the strips in a mixing bowl and add the cognac. Let stand until ready to use.

3. Preheat the oven to 350 degrees.

4. It is preferable to grind the pork and pork liver by hand, although this may be done by the butcher or in a blender. We use a heavy, number 10 hand grinder fitted with a fine or medium blade.

5. Put the ground pork and liver mixture in a mixing bowl and add the eggs, cream, and spices. Add mushroom-onion mixture and the cognac from the ham. Pick over the chicken livers, removing excess fat and membrane, and cut them into ½-inch cubes. Fold the chicken liver pieces into the pork mixture and add salt and pepper to taste.

6. Spoon about one-third of the mixture into a 2-quart loaf pan or soufflé dish. Arrange half the ham strips over the pork mixture in parallel lines about 1 inch apart. Scatter half the pistachios over that. Add another third of the pork mixture, the remaining ham, and remaining pistachios. Add the remaining pork mixture and smooth the surface. You may decorate the surface with bay leaves if you wish. Cover closely with aluminum foil and tie with string. (See note.)

7. Place the dish in a larger dish or baking pan and add boiling water to a depth of about 1 inch or more around the pâté dish. Place the dish in its water bath in the oven and bake exactly 2 hours or until the temperature in the center of the pâté registers 160 degrees on a meat thermometer. Remove the dish from the oven and remove the aluminum foil. While still hot, weight the pâté down with something clean, flat, and heavy. This will give better body to the pâté. Let the weights stand until the pâté is cool. Unmold. Serve with watercress sprigs around it. Serve sliced with a crusty French or Italian loaf or buttered toast. Cornichons, small sour gherkins, preferably imported, are traditionally served with pâtés. Closely covered leftover pâté will keep for a week or longer in the refrigerator.

Note: If you have any pork mixture left over, you can shape it into patties and fry, or fit it into a smaller container and make a second pâté.

13

*Russia*

## Piroshki

*(Meat-filled dumplings)*

Yield: About 45 piroshki

Dough
| | |
|---|---|
| 1½ | cups milk |
| 4 | tablespoons butter |
| 1 | envelope dry yeast |
| ⅓ | cup warm water |
| 3 | tablespoons sugar |
| 4—5 | cups unbleached flour |
| 1 | tablespoon salt or to taste |
| 3 | eggs, lightly beaten |

Filling
| | |
|---|---|
| 2 | pounds ground chuck, cooked until tender (see recipe for beef broth) |
| ⅓ | cup oil |
| 2 | cups finely chopped onion |
| | Salt and freshly ground black pepper |
| 4 | tablespoons butter |
| 1 | pound fresh mushrooms, cut into very fine dice or chopped |
| ¼ | cup finely chopped dill |

1. To prepare the dough, put the milk in a saucepan and bring just to the boil. Remove from the heat and add the 4 tablespoons butter. Let stand until the butter melts and the mixture is just warm.

2. Combine the yeast with the water and ¼ teaspoon of sugar. Stir to dissolve the yeast.

3. Measure out 4 cups of flour into a large bowl

and add the remaining sugar and the salt. Stir. Make a well in the center and add 2 eggs, warm milk and butter mixture, and the yeast. Start combining the flour with the center liquid ingredients, working rapidly and beating with a wooden spoon until well blended. Scoop out onto a floured board and start kneading. Add more flour, up to 1 more cup, until the dough is smooth and no longer sticky. Add the flour about ¼ cup at a time. Gather the dough into a ball. Rub a warm bowl with butter and add the ball of dough.

4. Cover the dough with plastic wrap and let rise in a warm place until double in bulk, about 1½ hours. Punch down in bowl and let rise again about 1 hour.

5. Meanwhile, to make the filling, grind the beef, using the fine blade of a food grinder. There should be about 4 cups.

6. Heat the oil in a skillet and add the onions. Cook until golden brown and add the beef. Blend well, adding salt and pepper to taste.

7. Heat the butter in another skillet and add the mushrooms, salt and pepper to taste. A good deal of liquid will come from the mushrooms. Cook this down briefly. The mixture should not be very dry. Add this to the meat mixture. Add the chopped dill. Blend well.

8. Preheat oven to 350 degrees.

9. Turn the dough out onto a lightly floured board when it is ready. Knead it briefly and divide it into 4 parts. Work 1 part at a time and keep the remainder covered. Roll out 1 piece at a time into a long, snakelike rope. Cut this off into 1½-inch lengths. Roll each piece into a ball and flatten with the fingers, turning it around and around into a 3-inch circle. Add to each circle 1 level teaspoon of filling. Fold the dough over to enclose the meat. Press around the edges to seal, tucking the pointed edges under. Place on a baking sheet. Continue making piroshki until all the dough and filling are used. Brush with remaining beaten egg and bake 25 minutes. Serve hot. These are also good cold and can be reheated.

*United States*

## Oysters Rockefeller

*Yield: 6 or more servings*

| | |
|---|---|
| 36 | oysters |
| 1 | pound or 2 10-ounce packages fresh spinach |
| 1 | cup finely chopped scallions |
| ½ | cup finely chopped celery |
| ½ | cup finely chopped parsley |
| 1 | clove garlic, finely minced |
| 1 | 2-ounce can anchovies, drained |
| 8 | tablespoons butter |
| 1 | tablespoon flour |
| ½ | cup heavy cream |
| | Tabasco |
| 1—2 | tablespoons Pernod or Ricard or other anise-flavored liqueur |
| ⅓ | cup grated Parmesan cheese |

1. Preheat oven to 450 degrees.

2. Open the oysters, leaving them on the half shell and reserving the oyster liquor.

3. Pick over the spinach and remove any tough stems and blemished leaves. Rinse well and put in a saucepan. Cover and cook, stirring, until spinach is wilted. Cook briefly and drain well. Squeeze to remove excess moisture. Blend or put through a food mill. There should be about 2 cups.

4. Put the scallions, celery, and parsley into the container of an electric blender and blend. There should be about 1 cup finely blended.

5. Chop the garlic and anchovies together finely.

6. Heat 4 tablespoons of butter in a skillet and add the scallion and celery mixture. Stir about 1 minute and add the anchovy mixture. Cook, stirring, about 1 minute, and add the spinach. Stir to blend.

7. Heat the remaining 4 tablespoons of butter in a saucepan and add the flour. Blend, stirring with a wire whisk, and add the oyster liquor, stirring vigorously with the whisk. Stir in the cream. Season with Tabasco to taste. Do not add salt. Add the spinach mixture and Pernod. Let cool.

8. Spoon equal portions of the mixture on top of the oysters and smooth over the tops. Sprinkle with Parmesan cheese. Bake about 25 minutes or until piping hot.

Note: The same spinach topping is equally as good (some think better) with clams on the half shell (clams Rockefeller).

*France*

## Asparagus with Sauce Vinaigrette

*Yield: 8 servings*

| | |
|---|---|
| 48 | asparagus spears |
| | Salt |
| 1 | tablespoon wine vinegar |
| 1 | tablespoon prepared mustard, preferably Dijon or Düsseldorf (do not use the baseball park variety) |
| | Freshly ground black pepper |
| ½ | cup peanut, vegetable, or corn oil |
| 1 | tablespoon finely chopped shallots or green onions |
| 1 | hard-boiled egg, sieved |
| 1 | tablespoon finely chopped parsley |

1. Use a potato peeler and scrape the asparagus spears to within about 2 inches of the top. Cut off and discard the tough bottoms of the spears to make them of uniform length. Place them in a skillet, add cold water to cover and salt. Bring to the boil and simmer until tender yet firm— 10 to 12 minutes or less.

2. Place the vinegar, mustard, salt and pepper in a mixing bowl and stir rapidly with a wire whisk. Gradually add the oil, stirring constantly. Stir in the shallots and half the sieved egg.

3. Drain the asparagus spears well while they are still hot. Plunge briefly into cold water to keep their color. Arrange 6 spears on each of 8 serving dishes. Spoon the sauce over the tips of the asparagus which should be lukewarm or at room temperature.

4. Blend the remaining egg with parsley and sprinkle it over the tips. Serve.

## **Funghi Ripieni con Spinaci e Acciughe**

*(Mushrooms stuffed with spinach and anchovies)*

Yield: 4 to 6 servings

- 1 pound mushrooms, preferably large ones (about 12 to a pound)
- 1 pound fresh spinach
- 1 2-ounce can anchovies
- 1 tablespoon olive oil
- 1/2 teaspoon chopped garlic
- 1/2 cup heavy cream
- 3 tablespoons melted butter
- 1/4 cup grated Parmesan cheese

1. Preheat oven to 400 degrees.

2. Remove stems and reserve the caps from the mushrooms. Chop the stems. There should be about 1 cup.

3. Pick over the spinach to remove any tough stems. Rinse the leaves well and drop them into boiling water to cover. Simmer about 1 minute and drain in a colander. Chill under cold running water and drain. Press the spinach between the hands to remove most of the moisture. Chop spinach. There should be about 1 cup.

4. Empty the oil from the anchovy can into a saucepan, adding a little olive oil, if necessary. Add the chopped mushroom stems. Cook, stirring, about 5 minutes and add the spinach and garlic. Chop the anchovies and add them. Stir to blend thoroughly. Stir in the cream and bring just to the boil. Remove from the heat and let cool.

5. Meanwhile, place the mushrooms, hollow side down, in a buttered baking dish. Brush with half the melted butter and place it in the oven for 10 minutes. Remove and let cool.

6. Stuff the cavity of each mushroom with the mixture, heaping it up and smoothing it over. Arrange the mushrooms in the baking dish and sprinkle with Parmesan cheese and the remaining melted butter. Place in the oven and bake 20 minutes.

## Crostini dello Chef
*(Toast with chicken-liver paste)*

*Yield: 8 to 12 servings*

| | |
|---|---|
| ½ | cup olive oil |
| ¼ | cup finely chopped onion |
| ¼ | cup coarsely chopped celery |
| ¼ | cup coarsely chopped carrot |
| ¼ | pound round of beef, cut into ½-inch cubes |
| ¼ | pound lean pork, cut into ½-inch cubes |
| | Salt and freshly ground black pepper to taste |
| ¼ | cup dry white wine |
| ¼ | teaspoon grated nutmeg |
| ½ | pound chicken livers, cut into ½-inch cubes |
| 3 | tablespoons drained capers |
| 3 | flat anchovy fillets, drained |
| 2 | teaspoons cognac |
| 2 | teaspoons dry sherry |
| 2 | tablespoons butter at room temperature |
| ½ | cup hot beef broth, approximately |
| 28 | slices French bread, each about ½-inch thick (see note) |
| | Olive oil |

1. Heat ¼ cup of oil in a saucepan and add the onion, celery, and carrot. Cook, stirring frequently, about 10 minutes until the onion is golden brown.

2. Add the beef, pork, salt and pepper and continue cooking about 15 minutes, stirring frequently.

3. Sprinkle with white wine and nutmeg and cook until wine is reduced, about 10 minutes, stirring frequently.

4. Add the chicken livers and cook, stirring occasionally, 15 minutes.

5. Add the capers and anchovies and cook about 10 minutes longer. Stir and add the cognac and sherry.

6. Remove the saucepan from the heat and add the butter. Stir over very low heat, gradually

adding about ¼ cup of broth. Add salt and pepper to taste. Spoon the mixture into the container of a blender or food processor and blend until smooth.

7. Preheat the oven to 400 degrees.

8. Arrange the slices of bread on a baking sheet and sprinkle or brush each slice with a little olive oil. Bake until crusty, 10 to 15 minutes.

9. Brush each slice with a little of the remaining beef broth and spread each slice with the paste.

Note: The number of slices depends on the size of the bread. The number indicated here is for a loaf about 2½ inches in diameter. If a large loaf is used, use half the number and cut each slice in half.

*Italy*

## Mussels alla Romana
*(Mussels with garlic and white wine)*

*Yield: 6 servings of 6 mussels each*

| | |
|---|---|
| 36 | mussels, well scrubbed |
| 2 | tablespoons or more olive oil |
| ½ | cup dry white wine |
| 1 | clove garlic, finely minced |
| ¼ | cup finely chopped parsley |
| | Hot red pepper flakes |

1. Wash the mussels well under cold running water and set aside.

2. Select a skillet large enough to hold the mussels in 1 layer. Add enough oil to barely cover the bottom of the skillet. Add the mussels and cover.

3. Cook, shaking the skillet until the mussels open, 3 minutes or longer. Throw away any mussels that don't open. Remove from the heat.

4. Pour the pan juices into a saucepan. Add the wine, garlic, and parsley and bring to the boil. Reduce by about half.

5. Meanwhile, remove and discard the top shell from each mussel. Place the mussels on the half shell in a bowl and pour the wine mixture over them. Sprinkle with red pepper flakes and chill.

## **Quiche Alsace**

*(Alsatian meat pie)*                    *Yield: 6 to 8 servings*

    Alsatian pastry for 1 10-inch pie
    (see recipe)
- 1   pound lean leg or shoulder of veal, ground, or use an equal quantity of ground lean pork
- 1/8   pound ground lean pork (in addition to the above meat)
    Salt and freshly ground pepper
- 1/8   teaspoon freshly grated nutmeg
- 2   teaspoons butter
- 1 1/2   tablespoons finely chopped shallots
- 1/3   cup finely chopped onion
- 3/4   cup finely chopped mushrooms (about 1/8 pound)
- 1   egg
- 1   egg yolk
- 1   cup heavy cream

1. Line a 10-inch tart tin (preferably a black, fluted-edge quiche pan with a removable bottom) with the pastry and chill it.

2. Preheat oven to 375 degrees.

3. Sprinkle the veal and/or pork with salt and pepper to taste and the nutmeg.

4. Heat the butter in a skillet and add the shallots and onion. Cook, stirring, until wilted and add the mushrooms. Cook 5 minutes, stirring frequently. Add the meat, stirring and breaking up lumps of meat with the side of a large metal spoon. Cook until most of the liquid is given up.

5. Beat the egg and yolk with a fork until well blended. Add the cream and salt and pepper to taste. Blend well and add the mixture to the meat. Stir well.

6. Pour the mixture into the prepared pie shell and bake 15 minutes. Reduce the oven heat to 350 degrees. Bake 30 to 35 minutes longer or until the custard is set. Remove from the oven and let stand. Serve lukewarm or at room temperature.

## Alsatian Pastry

*Yield: Enough for 10-inch tart*

2½    cups flour
¼    pound butter
    Salt
6    tablespoons well-chilled corn oil
6    tablespoons cold milk, approximately

1. Put the flour in a mixing bowl and place it in the freezer. Place the butter in the freezer and let both stand ½ hour or longer.

2. Remove the flour and cut the butter into bits, adding it to the flour. Add salt to taste. Using the fingers or a pastry blender, cut the butter into the flour until the mixture is like coarse corn-meal.

3. Gradually add the oil, stirring with a 2-pronged fork. When blended, gradually add the milk, working the pastry with the hands until it forms a dough. Knead briefly and gather the dough into a ball. Wrap it in wax paper and chill at least 30 minutes.

4. Remove the dough from the refrigerator and place it on a lightly floured surface. Roll it out into a rectangle measuring about 12 by 6 inches.

5. Fold a third of the dough over toward the center. Fold the other side of the dough over toward the center, thus making a 3-layer package of dough. Cover and refrigerate about ½ hour.

6. Roll out the dough once more on a lightly floured surface, sprinkling the surface with additional flour as necessary. Roll it into another rectangle. Fold the dough into thirds as before, cover and chill. The dough is now ready to be rolled into a circle for fitting into the tart tin.

*Mexico*

## Corn Soup

*Yield: 6 servings*

3½   cups fresh corn, cut and scraped from
      the cob (about 8 to 12 ears, depending
      on the size of the ears)

 ¾   cup water

 ¼   cup butter

  2   cups milk
      Salt

  2   tablespoons canned mild green chilies
      (Ortega or El Paso brand), cut into cubes

  1   cup cubed white "melting" cheese, such
      as Monterey Jack, Muenster, or Fontina
      Granulated sugar (optional)

  6   or more tablespoons deep-fried tortilla
      squares (see note)

1. Use a knife or corn scraper (available in hardware stores) to cut off the kernels. After cutting, scrape the cobs for the remaining "milk."

2. Place the kernels, "milk," and water in the container of an electric blender. Blend briefly to break up the kernels, but do not overblend.

3. Put the blended mixture through a fine sieve, pressing to extract as much liquid as possible. Pour the mixture into a saucepan and add the butter. Simmer slowly 5 minutes, stirring well because the corn tends to stick. Add the milk and salt to taste. Bring to a boil and add the green chilies.

4. When ready to serve, add the cheese and sugar, and when the cheese is melted and the soup is piping hot, serve immediately in soup cups. Garnish each serving with the deep-fried tortilla squares.

Note: Stack 6 or 8 tortillas on a flat surface and use a sharp knife to cut them into cubes about ½-inch square. Drop the cubes into hot fat and cook, stirring with a wooden spoon, until crisp and golden.

**25**

## Cuba
# Sopa de Frijoles Negros
*(Black bean soup)*

*Yield: About 10 to 12 servings*

| | |
|---|---|
| 1 | pound dried black beans such as black turtle beans, soaked overnight |
| 1/4 | cup olive oil, preferably imported |
| 1/4 | pound salt pork, cut into 1/2-inch cubes |
| 2 | chorizos (Portuguese sausages) or 1 smoked pork butt |
| 4 | cups finely chopped onions |
| 1/3 | cup finely minced garlic |
| 14 | cups fresh or canned beef broth |
| | Salt and freshly ground black pepper |
| 1/4 | teaspoon cayenne pepper, more or less to taste |
| 2 | tablespoons wine vinegar |
| 1/4 | cup dry sherry |

## Garnish

Chopped onion
Thin slices of lime with peel on
Cooked rice

1. Rinse the beans well and pick them over to remove foreign particles if there are any. Place the beans in a mixing bowl and add cold water to cover to a depth of about 4 inches above the beans. Let stand overnight.

2. Heat the oil in a soup kettle and add the salt pork, the sausages or smoked butt, 4 cups chopped onion, and garlic. Cook, stirring, about 5 minutes until onions are translucent and salt pork has been rendered of its fat.

3. Drain the beans well and add them to the kettle. Add the broth and bring to the boil. Add salt, black pepper, and cayenne pepper. Partially cover and cook, stirring occasionally, about 4 hours. Remove the sausages, slice them, and return to the soup. (If you are using smoked butt, it should be cubed, then returned to the soup.)

4. Put half the soup with the beans through a food mill or sieve or blend in a blender. Return this mixture to the kettle and stir to blend with the remaining soup and beans. Add the vinegar and dry sherry. Serve piping hot with chopped onion, lime slices, and rice all in separate bowls.

## Misoshiru

*(Bean soup)*

*Yield: 3 servings*

| | |
|---|---|
| 3 | cups dashi (see recipe) |
| 1/3 | cup red miso (bean paste) available in Japanese food outlets |
| 1/8 | teaspoon monosodium glutamate, optional |
| 1/2 | cup thinly sliced fresh mushrooms |
| 2 | or 3 tablespoons chopped scallions for garnish |

1. Pour the dashi into a saucepan and add the miso. Work the miso into the dashi by stirring constantly. Taste the soup. If it is not strong enough, stir in a little more miso. If it is too strong or too salty, thin it with more dashi.

2. When ready to serve, strain the soup into another saucepan. Add the monosodium glutamate and mushrooms. Bring to the boil and pour equal quantities into 3 soup bowls. Garnish each serving with chopped scallions.

Note: Many ingredients can be added to this soup including bean curd cut into cubes (available in Oriental groceries) and shrimp.

## *Dashi*

*(Japanese soup stock)*

*Yield: About 5 cups*

| | |
|---|---|
| 5 | cups cold water |
| 1 | large square or rectangle kombu (kelp) measuring about 7 by 7 inches (see note) |
| 3 | cups (about 1 1/2 ounces) loosely packed packaged katsuobushi or dried bonito shavings (see note) |

1. Place the 5 cups of water in a saucepan and add the kombu. Bring to boil and immediately remove the kombu. Do not let the kombu cook.

2. Add the katsuobushi and stir. Remove from the heat immediately. Strain immediately through flannel.

Note: Both kombu and katsuobushi are available in Japanese markets.

*Indonesia*

## Soto Ajam

*(A Balinese chicken soup, a meal in itself)*

*Yield: 6 servings*

| | |
|---|---|
| 4 | small, waxy new potatoes |
| 2 | eggs |
| 2 | large cloves garlic, peeled |
| ¼ | cup water |
| 4 | thin slices fresh ginger or ½ teaspoon dried ginger |
| 1½ | teaspoons ground turmeric |
| 7 | black peppercorns |
| | Salt |
| 1 | tablespoon deep-fried garlic (see below) |
| ¼ | cup deep-fried onion (see below) |
| 8 | cups chicken broth or water, approximately |
| 2 | small whole chicken breasts or 1 large whole chicken breast, halved |
| | Vegetable oil for frying |
| 1 | djeruk purut leaf |
| ½ | teaspoon sereh |
| 1 | small package (2 cups loose) Japanese bean thread |
| ½ | cup finely chopped celery leaves |
| ½ | cup finely chopped scallions |
| 1 | lime, thinly sliced or cut into wedges |

1. Boil the potatoes in their skins until tender, then drain and let cool. Peel and set aside.

2. Simmer the eggs in water to cover for about 10 minutes, until hard-cooked. Peel and set aside.

3. Place the garlic cloves, water, ginger, tur-

meric, peppercorns, salt, deep-fried garlic, and half the deep-fried onion in an electric blender. Blend into a paste, then set aside.

4. Bring the chicken stock or water to a boil. If water is used, add salt to taste. Add the chicken breasts, making sure they are covered with liquid, and simmer, covered, skimming the surface as necessary, about 5 minutes for small breasts, 10 minutes for large. Drain; reserve the liquid.

5. Place the bean thread in a bowl and pour boiling water over it. Let stand until ready to serve, then drain.

6. Heat about ½ inch of oil in a skillet and add the chicken breasts, skin side down. Cover and cook until golden on one side, then turn the pieces, cover, and cook until done. Drain on absorbent towels. To prepare the chicken as a garnish, cut the meat, including the skin, into bite-sized pieces.

7. Meanwhile, simmer the liquid in which the chicken cooked. Spoon the pureed garlic mixture into the stock. Add the djeruk purut leaf and sereh. Cook, partly covered, about 20 minutes, skimming off all fat and foam from the surface.

8. When ready to serve, arrange the garnishes— the bean thread, chopped celery leaves, chopped scallions, the hard-boiled eggs cut into quarters, the potatoes, thinly sliced, and the fried chicken —on a large platter.

9. To serve, keep the soup boiling at the table. Let each guest place one or some of each item on the garnish platter into a hot soup bowl. Add the boiling broth. Serve the remaining fried onions as a garnish. Serve the lime separately, to be squeezed into the soup.

## Deep-Fried Onion or Garlic

To prepare an onion for deep frying, peel it and slice it into the thinnest possible rings. To prepare garlic cloves, peel them and slice them thinly. Drop the onion or garlic into hot fat and cook quickly, stirring, until golden brown.

*Spain*

## Gazpacho

*Yield: 6 servings*

| | |
|---|---|
| 3 | cups coarsely chopped, cored, fresh tomatoes |
| 1½ | cups coarsely chopped, peeled cucumber |
| 1 | green pepper, cored, seeded, and coarsely chopped |
| 1 | clove garlic, sliced |
| ½ | cup water |
| 5 | tablespoons olive oil or vegetable oil |
| ¼ | cup or more wine vinegar |
| | Salt and freshly ground black pepper to taste |
| 2 | slices untrimmed fresh bread, cubed |

### *Garnish*

| | |
|---|---|
| 1 | cup bread cubes |
| 1 | clove garlic, minced |
| 2 | tablespoons olive oil |
| 1 | cucumber, diced |
| 1 | onion, chopped or 4 scallions |
| 1 | green pepper, chopped |
| 1 | tomato, peeled and chopped |

1. In the container of an electric blender, combine all the ingredients, with the exception of the garnish. Blend on high speed, stirring down with a spatula as necessary.

2. When all the ingredients are blended, pour the mixture through a sieve or strainer. Press and stir with a wooden spoon to extract as much of the juices as possible. Discard the solids in the sieve. Taste the soup for seasoning and add more salt, pepper, and vinegar, if desired. Chill the soup thoroughly before serving.

3. Brown bread cubes in oil and garlic. Garnish each soup bowl with the croutons, cucumber, onion, green pepper, and tomato.

# Borscht

*(Cabbage and beet soup)*

*Yield: 12 or more servings*

| | |
|---|---|
| 5 | pounds beef bones, including shin and neck bones |
| 1 | 4—5-pound duck with giblets, liver, and neck |
| 5 | quarts water |
| 1 | large turnip (about 1/3 pound), peeled and quartered |
| 1 | clove garlic, unpeeled |
| 1 | large onion (about 1/2 pound), stuck with 4 cloves |
| 4 | ribs celery with leaves, cut into 2-inch lengths |
| 1 | bay leaf |
| 6 | parsley sprigs |
| 3 | sprigs fresh thyme or 1/2 teaspoon dried |
| 2 | carrots, scraped and cut into 2-inch lengths |
| 1 | large fennel bulb with leaves (or fern) |
| | Salt |
| 16 | black peppercorns |
| 2½ | pounds short ribs of beef (3 or 4) |
| 2 | tablespoons butter |
| 3/4 | pound fresh raw beets, sliced, then cut into fine strips |
| 1 | pound red cabbage, finely shredded (about 8 cups) |
| 2 | carrots, scraped and cut into very fine 2-inch strips (about 1½ cups) |
| 4 | ribs celery, without leaves, cut into fine 2-inch strips (about 2 cups) |
| 4 | sweet Italian sausages |
| 3/4 | pound fresh raw beets, coarsely chopped |
| 2 | cups sour cream |

1. Place the beef bones in a kettle and add cold water to cover. Bring to the boil and simmer 5 minutes. Drain and run under cold water until the bones are chilled.

2. Put the bones in a clean kettle and add the duck neck, gizzard, and liver. Keep the duck refrigerated.

3. To the kettle add the 5 quarts of water, the turnip, garlic clove, onion stuck with cloves,

celery with leaves, bay leaf, parsley sprigs, thyme, and the carrots, cut into 2-inch lengths. Cut off the leaves or fern of the fennel bulb and chop enough to make 1 cup. Add the chopped leaves to the kettle. Add the salt and peppercorns and simmer 3 hours. Slice the fennel bulb and then cut into very fine matchlike strips. Set aside.

4. During the last hour of simmering, preheat the oven to 425 degrees. Sprinkle the beef ribs with salt and pepper and place them, bone side down, in a roasting pan.

5. Sprinkle the duck inside and out with salt and pepper and place it in another roasting pan, breast side up.

6. Place the beef ribs and duck in the oven and roast 15 minutes. Turn the ribs and the duck and continue roasting 10 minutes. Pour off the fat from both pans and set the ribs and duck aside.

7. Meanwhile, heat the butter in a deep saucepan or kettle and add the shredded fennel bulb, beets, shredded cabbage, carrots and celery. Sprinkle with salt and pepper and cook, stirring occasionally, about 15 minutes.

8. Strain the stock from the kettle into a clean utensil and discard the vegetables. Add the shredded vegetables cooked in butter to the stock and add the duck and beef ribs. Cook 1 hour and remove the duck. Set it aside. Continue cooking the soup with the ribs 30 minutes longer. Skim off all fat from the surface.

9. Meanwhile, place the sausages in a skillet and add 2 cups of the broth. Simmer, partially covered, about 15 minutes. Set aside.

10. Place the coarsely chopped beets in the container of an electric blender and add about a ½ cup cold water. Blend thoroughly. Line a sieve with cheesecloth and pour the mixture into it. Bring up the edges of the cheesecloth and squeeze it to extract as much beet juice as possible. Discard the solids.

11. When ready to serve, remove the meat from the beef ribs and the duck's carcass. Discard the

duck's skin and bones. Cut the duck meat and beef into bite-size cubes and add to the kettle. Cut the sausages thinly and add to the kettle. Bring to a boil.

12. When ready to serve, empty the sour cream into a mixing bowl and add salt to taste. Whip until smooth. Serve the raw beet juice and the sour cream on the side.

*British Isles*

## Scottish Broth

*Yield: 6 to 8 servings*

2   pounds neck bones of lamb
2   tablespoons butter
    Salt and freshly ground black pepper
1   cup finely chopped onion
1   clove garlic, finely minced
8   cups water
1   cup chopped celery
1½  cups diced white turnips or rutabaga
1   cup diced carrots
1   cup peeled, cored, and diced fresh
    tomatoes, or canned tomatoes
⅓   cup pearl barley
1   cup fresh or frozen green peas

1. In a large kettle, cook the neck bones in the butter, stirring, about 5 minutes. Add salt and pepper to taste.

2. Add the onion and garlic and cook, stirring, about 5 minutes. Add the water, and salt and pepper to taste. Bring to the boil and simmer, partially covered, about 45 minutes.

3. Add the celery, turnips, carrots, and tomatoes and simmer 30 minutes. Add the barley and cook 40 minutes. Add the peas and cook about 5 minutes longer or until the peas are tender. The total cooking time is 2 hours.

4. Remove the bones from the soup. Cut or pull off the meat from the bones and return it to the kettle. Discard the bones. Serve soup piping hot.

## United States

## **Manhattan Clam Chowder**

*Yield: 8 to 10 servings*

| | |
|---|---|
| 24 | chowder or razor clams |
| ½ | cup cornmeal |
| 4 | cups water |
| ¼ | cup cubed salt pork |
| 2 | cups finely diced carrots |
| 1½ | cups cubed celery |
| 2 | cups chopped onions |
| ¾ | cup chopped green pepper |
| 1 | clove garlic, finely chopped |
| 1 | teaspoon dried thyme |
| 1 | bay leaf |
| 1 | cup fresh or canned tomatoes, coarsely chopped |
| 4 | cups potatoes cut into ½-inch or slightly smaller cubes |
| | Salt and freshly ground black pepper |

1. Wash the clams well. If razor clams are used, they may be placed in a basin of cold water to which about ½ cup of cornmeal is added. Let stand about 1 hour to disgorge excess sand. Drain well and rinse thoroughly. Drain again.

2. Place the clams in a kettle and add the water. Simmer until shells open.

3. Meanwhile, chop the salt pork and put into a second kettle. Cook until it is rendered of its fat. Add the carrots, celery, onions, and green pepper. Cook about 5 minutes, stirring often.

4. Add the garlic, thyme, and bay leaf.

5. When the clams open, strain them but reserve both the clams and their liquid. Add the liquid to the salt pork mixture, adding enough water, if necessary, to make 10 cups. Add the tomatoes. Cook 15 minutes.

6. Remove the clams from the shells and discard the shells. Chop the clams finely on a flat surface or put them through a meat grinder, using the small blade. Add them to the kettle and add the potatoes. Add salt and pepper to taste and cook for approximately 1 hour.

*France*

## Cream of Watercress Soup

*Yield: 8 servings*

1   bunch watercress
6   tablespoons butter
1   cup coarsely chopped onion
4   medium potatoes (about 1½ pounds), peeled and quartered
4   cups chicken broth or 2 cups broth and 2 cups water
1   cup heavy cream

1. Wash and pick over the watercress, removing any tough stems. Set aside some individual leaves for a garnish.

2. Melt 4 tablespoons of butter in a large saucepan and add the onion. Cook until the onion has wilted. Add the watercress, potatoes, and chicken broth and bring to a boil. Simmer until the potatoes are quite tender. Put the soup through a food mill, sieve, or food processor, and return to the saucepan. Stir in the cream and bring to a boil. Remove from the heat and add the remaining butter. Garnish with shredded watercress leaves, serve immediately.

## Spain

# Fish Soup Valenciana

*Yield: 8 to 10 servings*

| | |
|---|---|
| ⅔ | cup olive oil |
| 2 | green peppers, cored, seeded, and chopped (about 2 cups) |
| 2½ | cups finely chopped onion |
| ½ | cup chopped leeks, optional |
| 1 | teaspoon fresh thyme or ½ teaspoon dried |
| 2 | bay leaves |
| 1½ | tablespoons finely chopped garlic |
| 1 | teaspoon chopped stem saffron, or to taste, optional |
| 1 | 2-pound, 3-ounce can Italian peeled tomatoes |
| | Salt and freshly ground white pepper |
| 3 | 2-pound live lobsters |
| 30 | shrimp, shelled and deveined |
| 30 | clams, well rinsed and drained |
| 1 | 3-pound cleaned striped bass (or use the equivalent of any white, nonoily, fresh ocean fish) |
| 10 | cups fish stock |
| ½ | pound pasta such as spaghettini, capellini, or vermicelli (or use spaghetti), broken into 3- or 4-inch lengths |
| 30 | mussels, scrubbed |
| | Tabasco |
| 3 | tablespoons Pernod or Ricard or another anise-flavored liqueur, optional |

1. Heat the oil in a large, deep kettle and add the chopped green peppers, onion, and leeks. Cook, stirring, about 5 minutes. Add the thyme, bay leaves, garlic, and saffron and cook, stirring, about 5 minutes.

2. Add the tomatoes, salt and pepper to taste and cover. Cook about 20 minutes, stirring occasionally.

3. Meanwhile, prepare the lobsters. Plunge a knife into the midsection where the tail and main body meet to kill them instantly. Sever the tail from the body and cut the tail section into 3 or 4 crosswise pieces. Pull off and discard

the tough sac near the eyes of the lobsters. Cut the body in half lengthwise, then cut each half in two. Do not remove the coral and liver, but leave intact.

4. Add the lobster pieces to the kettle and stir. Add the shrimp, clams, and fish. Add the fish stock and salt and pepper to taste. Cover and cook about 15 minutes.

5. Now, carefully remove the pieces of fish, shrimp, clams, and the tail pieces of the lobster to a large bowl. Cover with foil to keep warm.

6. Add the pasta to the kettle and cook about 5 minutes. Add the mussels and cook, uncovered, over high heat 15 minutes or until pasta has the desired degree of doneness. Note that pasta cooked in a tomato sauce requires longer cooking. Return the fish and seafood to the kettle and heat thoroughly. Taste for seasoning and add more salt and pepper if necessary, a touch of Tabasco, and the Pernod or Ricard.

Note: If 3 pounds or so of fresh squid is available, it may be cut into 2-inch lengths, after cleaning, and added to the soup about 10 minutes after the tomatoes are added.

## *Beef Broth*

*Yield: About 3 quarts*

| | |
|---|---|
| 2 | pounds chuck |
| 4 | marrow bones |
| 2 | carrots, scraped and quartered |
| 1 | onion, peeled and stuck with 4 cloves |
| 1 | parsnip, trimmed and quartered, if available |
| 3 | ribs celery, trimmed and quartered |
| 5 | quarts water |
| | Salt |
| 12 | black peppercorns |

Combine all the ingredients in a kettle and bring to the boil. Simmer 3 to 4 hours. Strain and reserve both the broth and the beef. Discard the vegetables. Skim surface to remove excess fat.

Note: Leftover beef broth can be frozen.

*Italy*

## Breaded Veal  Milan-Style

*Yield: 2 servings*

| | |
|---|---|
| ½ | pound veal scaloppine |
| | Flour for dredging |
| | Salt and freshly ground black pepper |
| 1 | egg |
| 1 | teaspoon water |
| 2 | tablespoons plus ½ teaspoon peanut, vegetable, or olive oil |
| ¼ | teaspoon grated nutmeg |
| ¾ | cup fresh bread crumbs |
| ¼ | cup grated Parmesan cheese |
| 2 | tablespoons butter |
| 2—4 | lemon slices |

1. Unless the scaloppine are very small, cut them into pieces measuring about 3 inches by 3 inches or slightly larger. Place them between sheets of wax paper and pound lightly to flatten, using the bottom of a heavy skillet or a flat mallet.

2. Season the flour with salt and pepper.

3. Beat the egg with the water, the ½ teaspoon of oil, and nutmeg.

4. Blend the bread crumbs with Parmesan.

5. Dip the scaloppine on both sides first in flour, then in egg, and finally in the bread crumb mixture. As the scaloppine are breaded place them on a flat surface and tap lightly to help the bread crumbs adhere.

6. Heat the butter and remaining oil in a heavy skillet and add the scaloppine. Cook until golden brown on one side, 2 to 4 minutes. Cook until golden brown on the other side. Serve hot with sliced lemon.

Optional: Garnish with capers and finely chopped hard-boiled egg whites and yolks.

## **Feijoada**

*(Meat and black bean stew)*

*Yield: 6 servings*

| | |
|---|---|
| 3 | cups dried black beans |
| | Water |
| 1 | pound carne seca (sun-cured salted beef) |
| 2 | pounds raw smoked tongue |
| ½ | pound linguica defumada (Portuguese sausage) |
| ½ | pound chuck beef |
| ½ | pound salt pork |
| | Salt and freshly ground black pepper |
| 2 | large cloves garlic, chopped |
| 2 | teaspoons shortening |

1. Wash the beans well and soak them overnight in water to cover. Soak the dried beef separately in water to cover. Drain the beans. Add 6 cups water and cook, covered, adding water as needed, until the beans are tender, or about 2½ hours. As soon as the beans are cooking, begin adding the other ingredients.

2. Cut the carne seca into 1½-inch squares and add to the beans.

3. Peel the tongue and cut it into large cubes. Cover with water and bring to a boil. Simmer 2 minutes, drain and add to beans.

4. Prick the sausages with a fork, cover with water, boil a few minutes, drain, and add to the beans.

5. Cut the chuck in half and add to the beans.

6. Cut the salt pork into ½-inch slices and add to the beans. Season the stew with salt and pepper.

7. When the beans are tender, brown the garlic lightly in the shortening. Add about 1 cup of the beans, mash and return to the large pot of beans. Adjust the seasonings.

8. Remove the pieces of meat to a hot platter and turn the beans into a chafing dish or bowl. Serve with braised pork loin, collards, onions in sauce (see recipes), sweetened orange slices, and hot rice. Cook the rice according to package directions, adding 1½ tablespoons shortening and

½ teaspoon vinegar for each 2 cups uncooked, long-grain rice.

## Braised Pork Loin

| 1 | pork loin (10-inch cut), about 4 pounds |
|---|---|
| 1 | lemon |
| 1 | clove garlic |
| | Tabasco |
| | Salt |
| ¼ | cup shortening |
| 1 | bay leaf |

1. Have the butcher bone the loin and reserve the bone rack. Rub the meat with lemon juice, garlic, Tabasco sauce, and salt.

2. Brown the loin in the shortening, turning to brown on all sides. Replace meat on bone rack and stand in a dutch oven.

3. Add the bay leaf and a little water to the pot, cover, and braise until tender, or about 1¼ hours.

## Collards

| 1 | tablespoon chopped onion |
|---|---|
| 2 | tablespoons shortening |
| 1½ | pounds collards, finely shredded |
| | Salt |

1. Sauté the onion in the shortening until it begins to brown.

2. Add the collards and salt, and cook over low heat, stirring frequently, until the collards are tender, or about 15 minutes.

## Onions in Sauce

| 1 | large onion, sliced thin |
|---|---|
| ¼ | teaspoon salt |
| 3 | tablespoons Tabasco |
| 2 | tablespoons olive oil |
| 2 | tablespoons vinegar |

1. Cover the onion with boiling water, drain and rinse in cold water. Drain well.

2. Add the remaining ingredients and let stand at room temperature 30 minutes or longer.

## Daube de Boeuf au Chambertin

*(Beef stewed in Burgundy wine)*

*Yield: 12 or more servings*

| | |
|---|---|
| 1 | 6—7 pound boneless shoulder of beef or other boneless beef for stewing |
| ¾ | pound carrots, scraped and cut into 2-inch lengths |
| 12 | or more small white onions, about ¾ pound, peeled |
| ¾ | pound white turnips, peeled and quartered or cut into eighths, depending on size, optional |
| 4 | whole cloves garlic, peeled |
| 1 | sprig fresh rosemary or 1 teaspoon dried |
| 2 | sprigs fresh thyme or 1 teaspoon dried |
| 2 | bay leaves |
| 6 | sprigs fresh parsley |
| ¼ | teaspoon grated nutmeg |
| 1 | bottle Chambertin or other dry red Burgundy |
| | Salt and freshly ground black pepper |
| ½ | pound lean salt pork, cut into thin slices |
| 4 | tablespoons lard, bacon fat, or salad oil |
| ⅓ | cup flour |
| 1 | tablespoon butter |
| ¾ | pound mushrooms, thinly sliced or quartered if small |

1. Cut the meat into 1½-inch cubes.

2. Place the meat in a deep bowl and add the carrots, onions, turnips, garlic, rosemary, thyme, bay leaves, parsley, nutmeg, wine, salt, and pepper. Cover and let stand overnight in the refrigerator, stirring occasionally.

3. Preheat the oven to 400 degrees.

4. Drain the meat, vegetables, and herbs, but reserve the marinating liquid. Separate the meat and vegetables. Tie the herbs (parsley, bay leaves, etc.) in cheesecloth.

5. Drop the salt pork slices into cold water and bring to the boil. Blanch 3 minutes and drain.

6. In a heavy, wide, and deep casserole or dutch oven, heat the lard and add the meat, pork slices, onions, and garlic. Stir and cook over

high heat about 15 minutes.

7. Sprinkle the meat with flour and stir thoroughly so that the flour coats the meat and other ingredients. Add the marinating liquid and stir. Add the herbs in cheesecloth. Cover and bring to the boil on top of the stove. Place the casserole in the oven and bake.

8. Heat the butter in a saucepan and add the sliced mushrooms. Cook until lightly browned. Add them to the stew. Cook about 45 minutes and add the turnips and carrots. Continue baking about 1 hour longer. The total baking time once the kettle is placed in the oven is 2 hours.

9. Remove the casserole and uncover. Carefully spoon off and discard all the fat from the top of the stew. Serve piping hot with buttered boiled potatoes, pureed potatoes, noodles, or rice.

*Belgium*

## Côtes de Veau aux Endives
*(Veal chops with endive)*

Yield: 4 servings

| | |
|---|---|
| 4 | loin veal chops, about ½ pound each |
| | Salt and freshly ground black pepper |
| ¼ | cup flour |
| 4 | tablespoons butter |
| 4 | firm, white, unblemished heads of Belgian endive |
| 2 | tablespoons water |
| 2 | tablespoons finely chopped shallots |
| 3 | tablespoons cognac |
| 1½ | cups heavy cream |
| ¼ | cup grated Parmesan cheese |

1. Sprinkle the chops on both sides with salt and pepper. Dredge lightly on both sides in flour.

2. Heat 3 tablespoons butter in a heavy skillet large enough to hold the chops in one layer. Cook chops over moderately low heat 8 to 10 minutes and turn. Cook, uncovered, 10 minutes longer.

3. While the chops are cooking, place the endive in a heavy saucepan. Add the remaining tablespoon of butter, salt and pepper, and the water. Cover closely and simmer 25 minutes. Take care that they do not burn. If necessary, add a bit more water.

4. When the chops are done, transfer them to a warm platter and cover with foil.

5. Add the shallots to the skillet and cook, stirring with a wooden spoon, for 30 seconds. Add the cognac and flame it. Stir with the spoon to dissolve the brown particles that cling to the bottom and sides of the skillet. Add the cream and cook, stirring, over high heat. Cook about

5 minutes or until the cream is thick and smooth. Strain the sauce into a saucepan and add salt and pepper to taste.

6. Preheat oven to 400 degrees.

7. Arrange the chops in one layer in an oval gratin or baking dish. Press the endive gently to remove any excess liquid. Arrange them around the chops. Spoon the sauce over all and sprinkle with the cheese. Bake, uncovered, 15 minutes.

*Haiti*

## Riz au Djon-Djon
*(Rice with black mushrooms)*

*Yield: 6 or more servings*

| | |
|---|---|
| 2 | cups dried black Haitian mushrooms (see note) |
| 2½ | cups cold water |
| 2 | slices bacon, cut into ¼-inch pieces |
| 1 | or 2 cloves garlic, finely chopped |
| 2 | tablespoons peanut or corn oil |
| | Salt |
| ½ | teaspoon red pepper flakes, more or less to taste |
| 2 | whole cloves |
| 2 | sprigs fresh summer savory, optional |
| ½ | small onion, thinly sliced (about ½ cup) |
| 1¾ | cups raw rice |

1. Pick over the mushrooms to remove any very tough and relatively large stems.

2. Put the water in a saucepan and add the mushrooms. Let soak 2 hours.

3. Add the bacon pieces, garlic, oil, salt, and pepper flakes to the mushrooms. Bring to the boil and add the cloves, savory, and onion.

4. Stir in the rice and bring to the boil.

5. Cut out a round of paper, preferably from an ordinary brown paper bag, slightly larger than the circumference of the saucepan. Cover with the paper round, then with a lid. Cook 30 to 35 minutes or until rice is tender.

Note: The mushrooms known as djon-djon in Haiti are available at Spanish markets.

*Hungary*

## Veal Goulash

*Yield: 8 or more servings*

| | |
|---|---|
| 2 | tablespoons lard, salad oil, or butter |
| 4 | cups halved and sliced onion, about 1 pound |
| 4 | pounds boneless veal, cut into 2-inch cubes |
| 1—3 | tablespoons paprika (see note) |
| 2 | tablespoons finely chopped garlic |
| | Salt and freshly ground black pepper |
| 2 | tablespoons flour |
| 2½ | cups chicken broth or 2 cups chicken broth and ½ cup dry white wine |
| 1½ | cups cored and seeded green peppers, cut into 1-inch strips |
| 1 | cup sour cream at room temperature, optional |

1. Preheat oven to 350 degrees.

2. Heat the lard in a dutch oven or deep, heavy saucepan and add the onion. Cook, stirring, until wilted. Add the veal and stir. Cook, stirring often, until the veal loses its red color.

3. Sprinkle with the paprika and stir. Cook 5 minutes and sprinkle with garlic, and salt and pepper to taste. Stir briefly and sprinkle with flour. Stir to coat the pieces of meat and add the chicken broth and wine. Bring to the boil. Cover with a round of wax paper and put the lid on. Place in the oven and bake about 1½ hours. Cooking time will depend on the quality of the veal. Best-quality veal cooks more rapidly than lesser quality.

4. Meanwhile, drop the green pepper strips into boiling water and blanch about 15 seconds. Drain immediately and set aside.

5. Thirty minutes before the stew is fully cooked sprinkle with the pepper strips. Continue cooking 30 minutes or until veal is tender.

6. If desired, add the sour cream. Preferably, it should be beaten with a whisk before adding and stirred in gradually. Serve the stew, if desired, with spaetzle (see recipe).

Note: The best Hungarian paprika is available in bulk. It comes in three strengths: sweet, medium, and hot. It should be added to taste.


## *Spaetzle*
*(Egg dumplings)*

Yield: 4 to 6 servings

| | |
|---|---|
| 2 | cups sifted flour |
| 3 | eggs |
| 2/3 | cup milk |
| | Salt |
| 1/8 | teaspoon grated nutmeg |
| 2 | tablespoons butter |

1. Place the flour in a mixing bowl. Beat the eggs and add them to the flour, stirring with a wire whisk or an electric beater. Gradually add the milk, beating or stirring constantly. Add salt and nutmeg.

2. Bring a large quantity of water to a boil in a kettle and add salt. Pour the spaetzle mixture into a colander and hold the colander over the boiling water. Press the mixture through the holes of the colander with a rubber spatula or large spoon. Or use a spaetzle machine and put the noodle mixture through, following the manufacturer's directions. The spaetzle are done when they float on the top. Drain the noodles and spoon them onto a clean towel or paper towels to dry briefly.

3. Heat the butter in a skillet and when it is hot, add the spaetzle, tossing and stirring 3 to 5 minutes. Serve hot.

## Rigatoni al Forno

*(Noodles with mushrooms, sausage,
and mozzarella)*

*Yield: 8 to 12 servings*

| | |
|---|---|
| 7 | tablespoons butter |
| 2 | cups finely chopped onion |
| 1 | pound mushrooms |
| 1 | pound ground pork or Italian sausages |
| 1 | teaspoon finely minced garlic |
| 3/4 | teaspoon fennel seeds |
| 1 | tablespoon finely chopped fresh basil or 1 teaspoon crushed dried |
| 3/4 | teaspoon crushed sage |
| 3/4 | teaspoon crushed oregano |
| 1 | dried red pepper, chopped (optional) |
| 6 | cups canned peeled Italian plum tomatoes |
| | Salt and freshly ground black pepper |
| 1 | cup water |
| 1 | cup chicken broth |
| 1/4 | cup finely chopped parsley |
| 2 | tablespoons olive oil |
| 1 | pound pasta—rigatoni or ziti |
| 1/2 | pound mozzarella cheese, cut into 1/2-inch cubes |
| 2 | cups grated Parmesan cheese |

1. Heat 3 tablespoons butter in a heavy large casserole and add the onion. Cook, stirring, until wilted.

2. If the mushrooms are tiny, leave them whole. Otherwise, quarter them or slice them, depending on size. Add the mushrooms to the onions and cook, stirring frequently, until the mushrooms give up their liquid. Cook further until the liquid evaporates.

3. In a separate skillet, add the pork. Or if sausages are used, split and pull off the skin. Add the sausage meat to the skillet. Cook, using a kitchen spoon to break up any lumps. Cook until the meat has rendered its fat. Pour off the fat. Add the meat to the mushroom mixture and stir it in. Sprinkle with garlic, fennel (omit the fennel if sausages are used), basil, sage, oregano, and red pepper. Cook about 3 minutes, stirring. Add the tomatoes, salt, pepper, water, and

chicken broth. Simmer 1 hour, stirring frequently.

4. Add the chopped parsley and simmer 15 minutes longer. Stir in the olive oil and set aside to cool.

5. Drop the pasta or ziti into a large quantity of boiling salted water and cook, stirring rapidly to make certain that the pieces of pasta float freely and do not stick to the bottom. Stir from the bottom. Cook about 8 minutes. Do not cook longer, for the pasta will be baked later. Immediately drain the pasta into a colander and run cold water over it. Drain well.

6. Preheat the oven to 400 degrees.

7. Spoon a thin layer of sauce into a 13½-by-8¾-by-1¾-inch baking dish. Add a single layer of rigatoni, scatter over it half the mozzarella and sprinkle with a tablespoon or so of Parmesan cheese. Continue making layers of sauce, pasta, mozzarella and Parmesan, ending with a layer of sauce and Parmesan for the dish. The remaining Parmesan will be served with the dish.

8. Dot the casserole with the remaining butter and bake, uncovered, for 30 minutes or until bubbling hot throughout. Run the dish briefly under the broiler to give it a nice brown glaze. Serve the dish cut into squares with Parmesan cheese on the side.

# **Poulet Sauté au Vinaigre**
*(Sautéed chicken with vinegar)*

Yield: 6 servings

| | |
|---|---|
| 2 | chickens, about 3½ pounds each, cut into serving pieces |
| | Salt and freshly ground black pepper |
| 4 | tablespoons butter |
| 6 | whole, peeled cloves garlic |
| 6 | whole, unpeeled cloves garlic |
| ½ | cup red wine vinegar |
| ¾ | cup dry white wine |
| 1 | cup fresh or canned chicken broth |
| 3 | tablespoons tomato paste |
| 1 | pound fresh, red, ripe tomatoes, peeled, seeded, and cut into 1-inch dice, about 2 cups |
| 2 | tablespoons tarragon wine vinegar |
| 3 | tablespoons chopped fresh tarragon or 1 tablespoon dried |

1. Preheat the oven to 400 degrees.

2. Sprinkle the chicken pieces with salt and pepper.

3. Heat equal amounts of the butter in 2 heavy skillets and add the chicken pieces skin side down. Brown on one side, 6 to 8 minutes, and turn. Add equal amounts of peeled and unpeeled garlic to both skillets. Cook the chicken, turning the pieces often, about 10 minutes. Using a slotted spoon, transfer the chicken from one skillet to the other. Pour off and discard the fat from the first skillet. Place the skillet containing all the chicken in the oven, uncovered. Let bake 10 minutes. Remove from the oven and cover.

4. Meanwhile, add the red wine vinegar to the first skillet, stirring to dissolve the brown particles that cling to the bottom and sides of the pan. Cook over high heat until reduced by half and add the wine and chicken broth. Add the tomato paste and stir to dissolve.

5. Cook about 15 minutes and add the tomatoes and tarragon wine vinegar. Bring to the boil over high heat and cook 10 minutes. Add the tarragon and cook about 3 minutes.

6. Pour off the fat from the skillet containing all

the chicken. Pour the tomato and tarragon sauce over the chicken and stir to blend. Bring to the boil stirring, and make sure the chicken pieces are well coated. Serve.

France

## Omelette Paysanne
*(Potato and sorrel omelet)*

Yield: 2 to 4 servings

| | |
|---|---|
| ⅓ | pound salt pork |
| 2 | tablespoons butter |
| 1 | cup finely shredded, loosely packed sorrel |
| 1 | medium-size baking potato, peeled and cut into ½-inch cubes (or slightly smaller), about 1 cup |
| ¼ | cup peanut, vegetable, or corn oil |
| | Salt and freshly ground black pepper |
| 6 | eggs |
| ¼ | cup finely chopped parsley |

1. Cut the salt pork into thin strips, each about the size of a paper match. These strips are called lardons. Put them in a small saucepan and add cold water to cover. Bring to the boil and simmer about 1 minute. Drain thoroughly.

2. Put the lardons in a small skillet and cook, stirring, until crisp. Drain well on absorbent paper toweling.

3. Heat 1 tablespoon of butter in a small saucepan and add the sorrel, stirring. Cook, about 30 seconds, until wilted.

4. Heat the oil in a small saucepan and add the cubed potato. Add salt and pepper to taste and cook over high heat, stirring and shaking the skillet, until the potatoes are crisp and brown, about 5 minutes.

5. Beat the eggs with salt and pepper to taste. Add the parsley and the sorrel.

7. Heat the remaining butter in an omelet pan or Teflon-lined skillet and add the lardons and potatoes. Add the egg mixture, stirring. Cook until omelet is set. Invert the omelet onto a hot round platter and serve.

*China*

## Hunan Lamb

*Yield: 6 to 10 servings*

| | |
|---|---|
| 3 | pounds boned lean leg of lamb |
| ½ | cup peanut oil |
| 12 | cloves garlic, crushed |
| 12 | hot dried red chili peppers |
| 1 | 1-inch cube fresh ginger, thinly sliced |
| 2 | scallions, cut into 2-inch lengths |
| ½ | pound rock sugar (available in Chinese groceries and in some supermarkets) |
| 2 | tablespoons chili paste with garlic (available in bottles in Chinese groceries) |
| ¼ | cup dark soy sauce (see note) |
| 2 | teaspoons salt |
| 1 | tablespoon monosodium glutamate, optional |
| 2¼ | cups beer |

1. Cut the lamb into 2-inch cubes.

2. Bring to the boil enough water to cover the lamb. Add the lamb and cook about 3 minutes, stirring occasionally. Drain quickly and run under cold water until thoroughly chilled throughout. Drain.

3. Heat the oil in a wok or kettle until it bubbles and add the garlic. Cook about 10 seconds and add the chili pepper and ginger. Cook over high heat until garlic and chili peppers are dark brown. Add the scallions and cook, stirring, about 20 seconds. Add the lamb and cook, stirring, about 1 minute. Add the rock sugar, chili paste with garlic, soy sauce, salt, monosodium glutamate, and stir to blend for 3 minutes or until the rock sugar dissolves. Transfer the mixture to a casserole and pour in the beer.

4. Cover the casserole and simmer gently until the lamb is tender, 45 minutes to an hour. Serve hot with rice.

Note: There are two kinds of soy sauce used in Chinese cookery. Thin or light soy is the most commonly found in supermarkets. Dark or heavy soy sauce, widely available in Chinese and other Oriental stores, has a greater viscosity.

**53**

## Couscous d'Agneau

*(A hearty Moroccan cereal-based lamb stew)*

*Yield: 8 to 10 servings*

| | |
|---|---|
| 1 | pound couscous (see note) |
| 10 | cups water |
| 8 | tablespoons butter, at room temperature |
| 4 | pounds cubed shoulder of lamb, other cuts may be used such as breast or leg, plus a few neck bones for flavor |
| 3 | leeks, optional |
| 6 | parsley sprigs |
| 1 | whole clove garlic, peeled |
| 1 | teaspoon grated fresh ginger or ½ teaspoon ground dried ginger |
| | Salt and freshly ground black pepper |
| 1 | tablespoon loosely packed stem saffron |
| 3 | carrots, about ½ pound, peeled and cut into ½-inch lengths |
| 14 | small white onions, about ½ pound, peeled |
| 3 | or 4 turnips, about ¾ pound, peeled and quartered or cut into sixths, depending on size |
| 3 | medium zucchini, trimmed and cut into 1-inch lengths |
| 2 | green peppers, about ½ pound, cored, seeded and cut into 2-inch squares |
| 1 | 1-pound, 4-ounce can chick peas, drained |
| | Hot pepper sauce (see recipe) |

1. Line a large bowl with cheesecloth. Add the couscous and sprinkle with 2 cups of cold water. Let stand 1 hour. Crumble the couscous with the fingers until all lumps are broken up.

2. Meanwhile, put 4 tablespoons of butter in a kettle or the bottom of a couscous cooker. Add the cubed lamb and turn the meat in the butter without browning. Tie the leeks and parsley sprigs together and add them. Add the garlic, ginger, salt and pepper. Finely chop the saffron and add it. Cook over low heat, stirring frequently, about 10 minutes. Add the remaining 8 cups of water, cover, and bring to the boil.

3. When the meat has cooked 15 minutes, place the fluffed couscous in a cheesecloth-lined colander or in the top of a couscous cooker. Place it on top of the kettle. It must fit snugly to steam

properly. Do not cover the couscous with a lid, but fold cheesecloth over it. Let the couscous steam 15 minutes.

4. Remove the couscous and its steaming utensil to the sink and sprinkle with ¼ cup of water plus salt to taste. Let it stand in the sink.

5. After the stew has cooked for a total of 30 minutes, add the carrots, onions, and turnips. Cook 15 minutes and add the zucchini and green peppers.

6. Cook 10 minutes and add the chick peas. Cook 5 to 10 minutes longer. While the chick peas are cooking, stir the couscous to break up lumps and let it steam again atop the kettle.

7. When ready to serve, empty the couscous into a hot bowl and add the remaining 4 tablespoons of butter. Stir to coat the grains. Serve the hot couscous with generous servings of meat and vegetables and hot pepper sauce on the side. Serve the hot broth in a sauce boat.

Note: Couscous is available in 1-pound packages in many food specialty shops in America.

## Hot Pepper Sauce

Place 2 or 3 tablespoons of cayenne pepper in a small bowl and add enough boiling water to make a thin paste. Add salt to taste. Serve at room temperature.

# Navarin des Homards

*(Baked lobsters with vegetables)*

*Yield: 14 servings*

| | |
|---|---|
| 1½ | cups small potatoes, peeled and quartered or cut into chunks |
| | Salt |
| ¾ | pound green beans, trimmed at the ends and cut into 1-inch lengths |
| 1 | cup shelled peas, the fresher the better |
| 1½ | cups carrots cut into bâtonnets (see note) |
| 1 | cup fresh turnips cut into bâtonnets (see note) |
| 3 | or 4 live lobsters, about 1–1½ pounds each |
| 6 | tablespoons butter |
| ¼ | cup olive oil |
| ⅓ | cup finely chopped shallots, about 8 |
| 8–10 | very small white onions, peeled and cut into quarters or eighths |
| | Freshly ground black pepper |
| ¾ | cup dry white wine |
| 1¼ | cups chicken broth, preferably freshly made |
| 3 | tablespoons flour |

1. Bring enough water to the boil in a saucepan to amply cover the potatoes. Add salt to taste and a bit more than seems necessary. Add the potatoes and cook until cooked but still a bit firm to the bite, about 10 to 15 minutes. Drain well.

2. Bring enough water to the boil in a saucepan to cover the green beans amply. Add salt as indicated above. Add the beans and cook until still a bit firm to the bite, about 10 to 15 minutes, depending on size and age. Drain and rinse under cold water until well chilled. Drain well.

3. Bring enough water to the boil to cover the peas thoroughly. Add salt as indicated above. Add the peas and simmer about 4 minutes or longer, until tender but still firm. Drain and rinse under cold running water. Drain well.

4. Combine the carrots and turnips and add cold water to cover. Add salt to taste and bring to the boil. Cook as above, about 10 minutes. Drain and rinse until cold. Drain well.

5. Plunge a knife into the center of each lobster where tail and body meet. This will kill the lobster instantly. Cut the lobsters in half at midsection between the carcass and tail. Cut the tail section into 3 pieces each. Cut the carcasses in half lengthwise. Remove and preserve the soft coral and liver section of the lobster. Discard the sac. Crack the claws.

6. Heat 4 tablespoons of butter and oil in a large, heavy casserole or dutch oven and add all the lobster pieces. Cook about 3 to 4 minutes. Add the shallots and onions and stir. Add the blanched vegetables — potatoes, green beans, peas, carrots and turnips. Add salt and pepper to taste. Cook, stirring, about 5 minutes to blend the flavors.

7. Add the wine and broth and cover. Cook about 10 minutes. Remove from the heat. Using a lid to hold the solids in place, drain off the liquid into a large, heavy saucepan. Bring liquid to the boil and let simmer about 15 minutes.

8. Meanwhile, add remaining 2 tablespoons butter to the coral and liver and blend well with the fingers. Add the flour and blend well. Add to the sauce, stirring vigorously. Bring to the boil and cook, stirring constantly, about 5 minutes.

9. Pour this mixture over the lobster mixture and bring to the boil. Cook, stirring, about 5 minutes. Serve.

Note: In French cooking, bâtonnets are vegetables that are cut the shape of tiny "batons." Vegetables cut bâtonnet-style include carrots, turnips, celery, and others that are first cut into any given small length, such as an inch or 2, and then cut into small rectangles about ¼ to ½ inch on all sides.

## Koenigsberger Klopse
*(Meatballs in caper sauce)*

*Yield: 8 to 12 servings*

| | |
|---|---|
| 1 | pound ground veal |
| 1 | pound ground pork |
| | Salt and freshly ground black pepper |
| 2 | whole eggs |
| 1 | hard roll, at least one day old |
| 1 | cup water |
| 10 | tablespoons butter |
| ¾ | cup finely chopped red onion |
| ½ | cup finely chopped parsley |
| 1¼ | teaspoons anchovy paste or more to taste |
| ½ | cup flour |
| 4 | cups fresh or canned beef broth |
| 1 | cup Rhine or Moselle wine |
| ⅓ | cup drained capers |
| 2 | egg yolks |
| ½ | cup sour cream |
| | Juice of ½ lemon |
| | Mashed potatoes, optional |

1. Combine veal, pork, salt, pepper, and 2 eggs. Soak the roll in water, drain and squeeze dry. Tear into small pieces and add to meat.

2. Melt 2 tablespoons butter in a saucepan and add the onion and parsley. Cook, stirring, until wilted and add to the meat. Add the anchovy paste and blend well.

3. Shape the mixture into 16 balls.

4. Melt the remaining 8 tablespoons butter in a saucepan and add the flour, stirring with a wire whisk. When blended, add the broth, stirring rapidly with the whisk. When blended and smooth, add the wine. Simmer 10 minutes.

5. Add the meatballs 1 by 1 to the sauce. Let cook 25 minutes, covered, occasionally stirring gently from the bottom to prevent sticking.

6. Remove the balls and add capers to sauce. Blend yolks with sour cream and stir in. Cook briefly over gentle heat without boiling. Add lemon juice, salt and pepper to taste. Add meatballs, heat gently. Serve with mashed potatoes.

*Germany*

## Choucroute Garnie

*(Baked sauerkraut with assorted garnishes)*

Yield: 6 servings with leftovers

| | |
|---|---|
| 4 | slices lean bacon |
| 2 | small onions, peeled and cut into thin slices |
| 1 | carrot, scraped and cut into rounds, about ¾ cup |
| 1 | clove garlic, halved |
| | Salt and freshly ground black pepper |
| 2 | sprigs parsley |
| 1 | bay leaf |
| 12 | juniper berries or 2 tablespoons gin |
| 3 | pounds sauerkraut |
| 1½ | cups dry white wine |
| 1 | cup fresh or canned chicken broth |
| 1 | 2-pound ready-cooked tongue |
| 6 | new potatoes, peeled |
| | Smoked meats |
| 1 | 2-pound smoked boneless pork shoulder butt |
| 2 | sprigs fresh thyme or ½ teaspoon dried |
| 4 | whole cloves |
| 1 | bay leaf |
| 1 | onion, thinly sliced |
| 1 | Polish ring sausage (kielbasa) |
| | Liver dumplings |
| ½ | pound pork liver |
| ½ | egg |
| ¼ | teaspoon grated nutmeg |
| | Salt and freshly ground black pepper |
| ¾ | cup fine fresh bread crumbs |
| 4 | tablespoons butter |

1. Preheat the oven to 400 degrees.

2. Cut the bacon into ½-inch strips. Scatter the bacon over the bottom of a 4-quart casserole

and cook over moderate heat, stirring until bacon is slightly rendered of its fat. Scatter the onions and carrot over the bacon and add the garlic, salt and pepper. Add the parsley sprigs, bay leaf, and juniper berries and cook, stirring, about 2 minutes.

3. Drain the sauerkraut (you may wash and drain it again if you wish). Add it to the casserole along with salt, wine, and chicken broth. Bring to the boil on top of the stove. Cover and bake in the oven 45 minutes, reducing the heat to 350 degrees. Add the tongue and potatoes. Bake 30 minutes longer or until potatoes are tender. (Total baking time is 1 1/4 hours.)

4. Meanwhile, prepare the smoked meats. Place the pork shoulder butt in a kettle and add water to cover. Add the thyme, cloves, bay leaf, and sliced onion. Simmer 1 hour and add the Polish sausage. Simmer 15 minutes longer.

5. While the other dishes cook, prepare the liver dumplings. Cut the liver into pieces and put them into the container of an electric blender. Add the egg and blend well. There should be about 3/4 cup blended. Put this through a fine sieve into a mixing bowl. Add the nutmeg, salt, pepper, and fold in the bread crumbs.

6. Bring 6 to 8 cups of water to the boil and add salt to taste. Using 2 spoons, one dipped in water after each use, scoop up a portion of liver mixture and, turning one spoon inside the other, drop oval-like dumplings into the simmering water. There should be about 6 dumplings. Simmer 6 to 8 minutes and drain on absorbent toweling. This can be done well in advance.

7. When everything is ready to be served, heat 4 tablespoons of butter in a skillet and cook the dumplings until golden brown on all sides, about 5 minutes.

8. Serve the sauerkraut along with slices or whole pieces of the drained smoked meats, the tongue, liver balls, potatoes, and so on. Serve with an assortment of mustards.

Note: Sauerkraut is good reheated. The meats are good cold or may be reheated.

*Vietnam*

## Grilled Lemon Duck

*Yield: 4 servings*

1    4½—5½-pound duck, quartered
4    scallions, trimmed and finely chopped
1    teaspoon grated fresh ginger
2    teaspoons powdered turmeric
2    tablespoons dark soy sauce (see note)
1    teaspoon sugar
     Salt and freshly ground black pepper
½    teaspoon grated lemon rind
     Lemon wedges
     Nuoc mam sauce (see recipe)

1. Quarter the duck or have it quartered. If the backbone is removed it will lie flatter on the grill. It will also cook more evenly if the wing tip and second wing bone are removed. Use a sharp knife and trim away all peripheral and excess fat.

2. Combine the scallions, ginger, turmeric, soy sauce, sugar, salt and pepper, and lemon rind. Rub the mixture into the duck. Let stand 4 hours or so, turning the duck pieces in the marinade.

3. Meanwhile, prepare a charcoal fire. Place the duck fat side down. Cook about 1 hour, turning the duck frequently and as necessary until it is

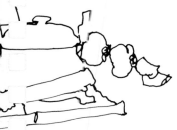

evenly cooked and the skin crisp. Serve with lemon wedges. Serve individual small bowls of nuoc mam sauce as a dip for the duck.

Note: The usual soy sauce served in America is light soy sauce. Dark sauce, a basic ingredient for Chinese cookery, is somewhat heavier both in color and density. It is widely available in Chinese groceries.

### Nuoc Mam Sauce

*Yield: About 1½ cups*

| | |
|---|---|
| 1 | cup fish sauce (see note) |
| 1 | tablespoon finely chopped peeled ginger |
| 2 | cloves garlic, finely chopped |
| 1 | teaspoon hot red pepper flakes or a little cayenne to taste |
| 3 | tablespoons lemon juice |
| 2 | tablespoons sugar |
| ¼ | cup water |

1. Combine all the ingredients and stir to blend. Serve equal portions into individual bowls and serve with Vietnamese dishes. Leftover sauce may be kept refrigerated for a week or longer.

Note: Fish sauce is widely available in Chinese groceries. A light soy sauce (preferably imported) such as that found on most American supermarket shelves may be substituted for the fish sauce.

*France*

## Striped Bass Fermière

*(Poached with vegetables and white wine)*

Yield: 8 servings

| | |
|---|---|
| 2 | skinless and boneless striped bass fillets, about 5½ pounds |
| 2 | or 3 small carrots |
| 15 | tablespoons butter |
| 1 | cup thinly sliced shallots |
| 1½ | cups thinly sliced celery |
| 4 | mushrooms, thinly sliced |
| 1½ | cups dry white wine |
| | Salt and freshly ground black pepper |
| | Juice of ½ lemon |
| 1 | cup heavy cream |
| | Parsleyed cucumbers (see recipe, page 87) |

1. Cut the fish fillets slightly on the bias into 8 steaks. Refrigerate.

2. Trim and scrape the carrots, and cut them into very thin rounds.

3. Select a heavy casserole large enough to hold all the pieces of fish in one layer. Add 8 tablespoons of butter. When it is hot, add the carrots, shallots, celery, and mushrooms. Add ⅓ cup of dry white wine. Cook until all the wine has been reduced, about 10 minutes. Add another ⅓ cup of wine and cook until it is reduced, about 10 minutes. Add another ⅓ cup of wine and cook until it is reduced, about 10 minutes. The total time for reducing wine is about 30 minutes.

4. Sprinkle the fish pieces with salt and pepper and arrange them in one layer over the vegetables. Pour the remaining ½ cup of wine over the fish and bring to the boil. Simmer about 6 minutes. Sprinkle with lemon juice.

5. Melt 2 tablespoons of butter in an oval serving dish large enough to hold the fish in one layer. Transfer the fish and cover to keep warm.

6. To the casserole add the cream and bring it to the boil over high heat, shaking the casserole so that the cream and the vegetable flavors blend, about 3 minutes. Add remaining 5 tablespoons of butter, bit by bit, while shaking the casserole. Pour this over the fish and serve immediately with parsleyed cucumbers. (see page 87)

## Murghi Masala

*(Chicken curry)*

*Yield: 4 to 6 servings*

- 1   3-pound chicken, cut into serving pieces
- 2/3   cup peanut, vegetable, or corn oil
- 1   large onion, coarsely grated, about 1½ cups
- 1   4-inch piece cinnamon stick
- 2   whole, cardamom seeds or ½ teaspoon ground cardamom
- 1   tablespoon finely minced garlic
- 1½–2   cups water
- 1   cup yogurt
- 1/3   cup fresh ginger, cut into thin strips or 1 tablespoon grated
- 1   teaspoon turmeric
- 2   teaspoons sweet paprika
- 1   teaspoon ground ginger
- ½   teaspoon ground cumin
- 1   teaspoon ground coriander
-   Salt
- ½   cup heavy cream

1. Pull off and discard the skin of the chicken or use the skin for soup. It is easy to skin the chicken, using the fingers and a dry clean towel for tugging.

2. Heat the oil in a large, heavy kettle and add the onion. Cook over medium heat, stirring, about 5 minutes until the onion is dry but not brown. Add the cinnamon and cardamom seeds and continue cooking, stirring, until onion is golden brown. Add the garlic and ¼ cup water.

3. Add the yogurt and cook briskly, stirring, about 5 minutes. Add the chopped ginger, turmeric, paprika, powdered ginger, cumin, coriander, and 1 cup of water.

4. Cook, stirring, about 5 minutes and add the chicken pieces. Add salt to taste. Cook 20 minutes, stirring frequently.

5. Add the remaining cup of water if necessary and cook about 10 minutes, stirring often. Add the cream and bring to the boil. Cook about 2 minutes. Serve hot with an Indian rice.

*Spain*

## Paella

*(Chicken, sausage and seafood stew)*

*Yield: 12 to 16 servings*

| | |
|---|---|
| 4 | 1—1½-pound live lobsters |
| 12 | tablespoons melted butter |
| | Salt and freshly ground black pepper |
| 3 | tablespoons olive oil |
| 1 | 3½-pound chicken, cut into serving pieces, including the liver and gizzard |
| 6 | sweet or hot Italian sausages, about 1 pound |
| 2 | medium-size onions, each cut into eighths |
| 8 | mixed sweet red and green peppers, each cored, seeded and cut into eighths (if red peppers are not available, use all green peppers), about 1 quart when ready to cook |
| 4 | large tomatoes, cored and quartered (about 1 quart loosely packed) |
| 2 | cloves garlic, coarsely chopped |
| 1 | tablespoon saffron or less to taste |
| 1½ | pounds raw shrimp, shelled and deveined |
| 24 | fresh mussels in the shell, scrubbed |
| 1 | dozen clams in the shell, scrubbed |
| 3 | cups raw rice |
| 3 | cups (approximately) chicken broth |

1. Preheat oven to 350 degrees.

2. Plunge a knife into the center of each lobster where tail and body meet. This will kill the lobster instantly. Cut the lobsters in half at mid-section, between carcass and tail. Cut the tail

section into 3 pieces each. Cut the carcasses in half lengthwise. Discard the sac. Crack the claws.

3. Arrange the pieces of lobster on a large baking dish and brush with butter. Sprinkle with salt and pepper and cover closely with foil. Place in the oven and bake for about 10 minutes. Remove the lobster pieces from the oven, set aside, and keep warm.

4. Meanwhile, select a large, deep skillet or use a traditional paella pan. Add the oil to the skillet and add the chicken and sausage and the onions. Cook over moderate heat, partly covered, turning the pieces occasionally until brown, about 20 minutes.

5. Add the red and green peppers, tomatoes, and garlic. Cook, uncovered, turning the pieces occasionally. Add the rice, stock, saffron, and salt and pepper to taste. Cover and cook about 15 minutes. Add the lobster, shrimp, mussels and clams. Cover once more and cook 10 to 15 minutes until the chicken is tender, the rice is done, and the clams and mussels have steamed open. Serve hot.

*British Isles*

## A Decidedly Delicious Way to Roast Beef

*Yield: 4 to 16 servings*

1   3½—8-pound eye round of beef roast
    Salt and freshly ground black pepper

1. Preheat oven to 500 degrees or its maximum setting.

2. Sprinkle the roast with salt and pepper. Outfit a shallow roasting pan with a rack and place the beef on it. Place the beef in the oven and bake exactly 4 or 5 minutes a pound. At the end of that time do not open the oven door. Let the roast remain in the oven from 1½ (for a small roast) to 2 (for a large roast) hours. The meat will be nicely browned on the outside and juicy within. If the meat seems too cool when removed from the oven, reheat it briefly in a hot oven before slicing.

## Perdrix aux Chou

*(Partridges with cabbage)*

*Yield: 8 servings*

| | |
|---|---|
| 2 | Savoy or green cabbages, weighing about 3 pounds each |
| 1 | pound unsliced bacon |
| 1 | cup thinly sliced onion |
| 1 | bay leaf |
| 1 | clove garlic, peeled and halved |
| | Salt and freshly ground black pepper |
| 4 | whole cloves |
| 2 | sprigs fresh thyme or ½ teaspoon dried |
| 4 | small white turnips, about ½ pound |
| 3 | whole carrots, about ½ pound |
| 4 | partridges |
| 2 | tablespoons butter |
| 1½ | pounds Polish sausage (kielbasa) |
| ⅓ | cup dry white wine |

1. Preheat the oven to 350 degrees.

2. Pull off and discard the tough outer leaves of the cabbages. Cut away and discard the core of the cabbages. Quarter the cabbages. Bring enough water to the boil to cover the cabbage pieces. Add the cabbage quarters and cover. Simmer 10 minutes. Drain and run under cold running water. Drain well.

3. Cut the bacon into 10 or 12 slices, each slice about ½ inch thick.

4. Line the bottom of a large, deep, heavy casserole with a single layer of bacon slices. Cook about 3 minutes on one side and turn the slices. Cook 3 minutes longer. The bacon should cook without becoming crisp or brown. Remove and reserve the bacon.

5. Add the onion slices to the bacon fat. Add the bay leaf, garlic halves, and cabbage quarters. Sprinkle with salt and pepper. Add the cloves, thyme, turnips, carrots, and cover with the reserved bacon slices. Cover and bake 1½ hours.

6. After the cabbage has baked about 1 hour, truss the partridges. Heat the butter in a skillet and brown the partridges on all sides. Bake uncovered, turning occasionally, about 20 minutes.

7. Add the kielbasa and partridges to the cabbage.

8. Add the wine to the skillet in which partridges cooked, stirring to dissolve the brown particles that cling to the bottom and sides of the pan. Add this to the cabbage. Cover and bake 30 minutes longer. Serve half a partridge, a bacon slice, sliced kielbasa, vegetables, and so on to each guest.

*Switzerland*

## Steak Tartare Lausanne

*Yield: 4 servings*

| | |
|---|---|
| 2 | pounds raw, ground top-quality beef fillet, sirloin, or round steak |
| 4 | raw egg yolks |
| 8 | anchovy fillets |
| | Capers |
| ½ | cup finely chopped onion |
| 4 | teaspoons chopped parsley |
| | Salt and freshly ground black pepper |

### Seasonings

| | |
|---|---|
| | Rose paprika |
| | Cayenne pepper |
| | Tomato ketchup |
| | Worcestershire sauce |
| 1 | lemon, quartered |
| | Prepared mustard |
| | Cognac or port to taste |
| | Buttered toast |

1. Divide the raw beef into 4 portions and shape into patties. Place the patties on chilled plates. Make a small indentation in the center of each and place 1 egg yolk in each.

2. Garnish each serving with 2 anchovies and sprinkle with capers, onion, parsley, salt and pepper to taste.

3. Serve immediately accompanied by the remaining seasonings and toast and butter. Each guest stirs the seasonings into his steak tartare according to his taste.

## Schweinebraten mit Senf

*(Roast loin of pork with mustard)*

*Yield: 6 to 8 servings*

| | |
|---|---|
| 1 | 4-pound loin of pork with bone |
| | Salt and freshly ground black pepper |
| ¼ | pound caul fat, sometimes called lace fat (see note) |
| ½ | cup imported mustard, preferably Dijon or Düsseldorf |
| 6 | sprigs fresh thyme or 1 teaspoon dried |
| 1 | onion, about ½ pound |
| 24 | very small white onions, peeled |
| ¼ | cup water |
| | Pureed lentils (see recipe) |

1. Preheat oven to 400 degrees.

2. Using a sharp knife, carefully trim away most but not all of the fat from the loin of pork. Sprinkle the pork with salt and pepper to taste.

3. Open up the sheet of caul fat on a flat surface. Place the pork, bone side down, in the center of the caul fat. Smear the mustard all over the pork. Arrange the thyme sprigs at various points over the pork. Or sprinkle with thyme if dried thyme is used. Bring up the edges of the caul fat to enclose the roast completely.

4. Place the roast, bone side down, in a roasting pan and bake, uncovered, 30 minutes.

5. Split the onion in half and thinly slice it. Scatter the slices around the pork. Arrange the small white onions around the roast.

6. Reduce the oven heat to 375 degrees and bake 45 minutes. Cover loosely with foil and cook 15 minutes longer.

7. Remove the foil and cover the roast with a heavy lid. Reduce the oven heat to 350 degrees and bake 30 minutes.

8. Remove the roast, leaving the juices in the pan. Remove the caul fat from the pork and transfer the roast to a serving dish. Use a slotted spoon and remove the small white onions. Spoon them around the roast as garnish.

9. Put the pan juices through a food mill or sieve into a saucepan. Skim off the fat. Bring the juices

to the boil and add the water. Bring to the boil again. Slice the roast and spoon a little of the sauce over each slice. Serve with lentil puree.

Note: Many pork stores carry caul fat or can order it for you. Unfortunately, there is no substitute for caul fat in this recipe.

## Lentil Puree

*Yield: 8 to 10 servings*

1 pound lentils
¾ pound potatoes, peeled and cut into eighths
1 small onion, stuck with 2 cloves
1 clove garlic, peeled
1 bay leaf
6 cups water
   Salt and freshly ground black pepper
1 cup heavy cream
4 tablespoons butter

1. Combine the lentils, potatoes, onion, garlic, bay leaf, water, salt, and pepper to taste in a saucepan. Bring to the boil and simmer 30 minutes or until the lentils are tender. Drain.

2. Pour the lentil mixture into a food press and pass it through into a saucepan. Discard any solids left in food press.

3. Add ¾ cup heavy cream, butter, and salt to taste. Beat well to blend. Smooth the surface and pour the remaining ¼ cup of cream on top to prevent a skin from forming. When ready to serve, heat thoroughly and stir to blend.

Note: Lentil puree makes an astonishingly good accompaniment to not only roast pork, but baked ham and almost any kind of sausage.

## Filets de Poisson aux Crevettes
*(Sole in white wine sauce with shrimp)*

Yield: 6 servings

| | |
|---|---|
| 5 | tablespoons butter |
| 2 | tablespoons finely chopped shallots |
| 8 | fillets of sole, striped bass, or other white-fleshed fish, about 2 pounds |
| | Salt and freshly ground black pepper |
| 2 | tablespoons finely chopped dill or parsley |
| ½ | cup dry white wine |
| ½ | pound raw shrimp, shelled and deveined |
| | A few drops Tabasco |
| 1½ | cups heavy cream |
| 1 | teaspoon lemon juice |

1. Preheat oven to 400 degrees.

2. Select a baking dish about 16 by 10 inches or large enough to accommodate the fish in one layer.

3. Grease the dish with 1 tablespoon of butter and sprinkle with the shallots. Place the fish, skinned side down, in 1 layer. Dot with the remaining 4 tablespoons butter and add salt and pepper to taste. Sprinkle with 1 tablespoon of dill and pour the wine over all. Cover closely with a piece of wax paper. Place the baking dish on top of the stove and bring the liquid just to the boil. Place the dish immediately in the oven and bake 5 minutes. Do not bake much longer, or the fish will become dry.

4. Meanwhile, place the shrimp on a flat surface and cut them into ½-inch pieces.

5. Carefully drain the liquid that has accumulated in the baking dish into a medium-size skillet. Add the shrimp, salt and pepper, and a dash of Tabasco. Simmer about 30 seconds. Using a slotted spoon, remove the shrimp and scatter them over the fish.

6. Reduce the cooking liquid over high heat about 2 minutes. Add the heavy cream and reduce it over high heat about 10 minutes or until the sauce is thickened. Add the lemon juice and a bit more Tabasco. If desired, add a little more salt and pepper. Spoon the sauce over the fish and shrimp and sprinkle with the remaining tablespoon of chopped dill. Serve with plain buttered boiled potatoes.

## **Canard Madagascar**
*(Duck with green peppercorns)*

*Yield: 8 servings*

| | |
|---|---|
| 2 | 4½—5-pound ducks |
| | Salt and freshly ground black pepper |
| ¼ | cup cognac or other brandy |
| 1½ | cups chicken broth |
| 2 | tablespoons tomato paste |
| 1½ | tablespoons green peppercorns (see note) |
| 1 | cup heavy cream |

1. The important thing about this recipe is to have the duck properly cut for cooking. Each duck should be cut into 4 serving pieces. Cut away the 2 breast halves from each carcass, but leave the main wing bone attached to each breast half. This will yield 2 boned breast halves with main wing bones attached. Leave the thighs and legs in 1 piece, but cut them off the carcass. Discard the carcass.

2. Do not skin either the breast or thigh sections, but cut away all peripheral fat that does not cover the flesh. Cut between the main wing bone and the second wing bone. Discard the second wing bone and the wing tip.

3. Sprinkle the 8 pieces with salt and pepper.

4. Heat a large, heavy skillet and add the duck skin side down. If 1 skillet is not large enough, use 2. It is not necessary to use butter or other fat because the duck's natural fat is enough. Cook the duck without turning about 15 minutes until golden brown, running a spatula beneath the pieces if necessary to prevent sticking. The important thing here is not only to brown the duck pieces nicely but to extract as much fat as possible.

5. Turn the pieces and cook 20 minutes longer.

6. Remove the duck pieces and pour off all fat.

7. Return the duck to the skillet or skillets skin side down. Flame them with the cognac. Add the chicken broth and tomato paste and stir to blend. Cover and cook 20 minutes.

8. Turn the pieces skin side up and cook uncovered 10 minutes longer. Scatter the peppercorns around the duck and add the cream.

9. Turn the pieces skin side down again and shake the skillet or skillets gently to blend the peppercorns and sauce. Cook 20 minutes longer. Serve with straw potatoes (see recipe, page 91).

Note: Green peppercorns can be bought at fine specialty stores.

*British Isles*

## Roast Pheasant

*Yield: 2 to 4 servings*

1    2—3-pound pheasant
     Salt and freshly ground black pepper
1    bay leaf
1    clove garlic
     Few celery leaves
1    slice lemon
4    slices bacon
     Melted butter
     Madeira sauce (see recipe)

1. Preheat oven to 350 degrees.

2. Sprinkle the pheasant inside and out with salt and pepper. Place the bay leaf, garlic, celery leaves, and lemon in the cavity. Tie the legs together with string and turn the wings under.

3. Cover the breast with bacon and a piece of cheesecloth soaked in melted butter. Place the pheasant, breast up, on a rack in a baking pan and roast until tender, about 30 minutes per pound, basting frequently with melted butter.

4. Remove the cheesecloth and string. If desired, serve the pheasant on a bed of rice accompanied by Madeira sauce.

### Madeira Sauce

Remove the pheasant to a warm serving platter and add 1 cup consommé to the pan. Stir over moderate heat, scraping loose the browned particles. Blend 2 tablespoons flour with 2 tablespoons butter and stir into the gravy bit by bit. When the gravy is thickened and smooth, add 2 to 3 tablespoons Madeira wine and the cooked pheasant liver, finely chopped.

## Yakitori
(Grilled fowl)

*Yield: dependent on quantity of chicken used*

Bone the chicken, setting aside the heart, liver, gizzard, etc. Cut the meat into bite-size cubes. Arrange the cubes on skewers. If desired, alternate 1- or 2-inch lengths of scallions with chicken on skewers.

Trim and cut away the tough, muscular parts of the gizzards if used. Arrange the tender gizzard pieces on skewers. Arrange the liver and heart on skewers. Grill the unseasoned chicken pieces, brushing as necessary with yakitori-no-tare (see recipe). Cook, turning often, until the chicken pieces are done. Remove from the heat, sprinkle with lemon and serve hot.

Note: Strictly speaking, only chicken or other fowl is used for yakitori, but you can use mushroom caps, asparagus wrapped in bacon, steak bits, and so on.

## Yakitori-no-tare
*(Sauce for yakitori)*

*Yield: About 2½ cups*

Chicken bones, optional
½ cup sake
½ cup mirin (sweet Japanese cooking wine)
⅓ cup or slightly more coarsely cracked rock sugar (see note)
1 cup dark soy sauce (see note)
2—3 tablespoons honey

1. If chicken bones are used, cook them over a charcoal fire turning often and without burning. Crack them and add them to a saucepan. Add the sake, mirin, rock sugar, and soy sauce. Bring to the boil and cook 3 minutes.

2. Stir in the honey and boil 2 minutes longer. Let stand. Strain before using.

Note: Rock sugar and dark soy sauce are available at many Oriental food shops.

## Skillet Teriyaki
*(Marinated and grilled sliced steak)*

*Yield: 4 to 6 servings*

½   cup soy sauce
½   cup mirin or dry sherry
1   teaspoon sugar
1   teaspoon ginger juice (see note) or
    ½ teaspoon ground ginger
2   pounds boneless sirloin or boneless
    shell steak
4   tablespoons unsalted butter

1. Combine the soy sauce, mirin or sherry, sugar, and ginger juice.

2. Cut off and discard any top fat on the meat and cut the meat into thin slices about a ¼ inch thick. Place the meat in a container and pour over it the soy sauce mixture. Let stand 5 minutes or longer. Drain the meat but reserve the marinade.

3. Use 2 skillets (or 1, if it's large enough) and heat 2 tablespoons of butter in each. Add the slices of beef and cook 30 seconds on one side; turn the pieces and cook 30 seconds on the other. When the meat is ready, transfer it to a warm platter. Add the reserved marinade sauce to one skillet and cook quickly about 1 minute. Pour the sauce over the meat and serve with plain unsalted rice.

Note: Ginger juice is made from grated fresh ginger. To make the ginger juice, break off a small piece of ginger and peel and grate it. Squeeze through cheesecloth.

## Saumon à l'Oseille
*(Salmon with sorrel sauce)*

*Yield: 4 to 6 servings*

| | |
|---|---|
| 1 | 3—3½-pound boned, skinned salmon or striped bass fillets |
| ¼ | cup chopped shallots |
| 4 | cups rich fish stock |
| 1½ | cups dry vermouth |
| 1 | cup dry white wine |
| 2¼ | cups heavy cream |
| | Salt and freshly ground black pepper |
| 3 | tablespoons fish glaze (see note), optional |
| ¼ | pound fresh sorrel stems removed |
| 4 | egg yolks |
| 2 | tablespoons butter |
| | Juice of ½ lemon |
| | Flour for dredging |
| ½ | cup clarified butter (see recipe) |

1. Cut the fish on the bias like smoked salmon into ¼-inch-thick slices. Flatten gently with a flat mallet. Refrigerate.

2. In a deep skillet, combine the shallots, fish stock, vermouth and white wine. Cook over high heat about 35 to 40 minutes until the liquid is reduced to about half a cup.

3. Add 2 cups cream, salt and pepper to taste. Bring to the boil and stir in the fish glaze, if used. Cook over high heat about 2 minutes. Cut the sorrel or spinach into very fine shreds (chiffonade). Add the sorrel or spinach and bring to the boil. In a bowl, beat the egg yolks with the remaining cream. Take 3 tablespoons of the hot sauce and mix it into the egg and cream. Remove the sauce from the heat and slowly stir the rest of it into egg and cream. Return the sauce to skillet and keep it hot over an asbestos pad. It will curdle if you let it boil. Add the 2 tablespoons butter and swirl it in. Season with lemon juice.

4. Keep the sauce hot but do not boil or it will curdle.

5. Dredge the fish slices lightly in flour seasoned with salt and pepper.

6. Heat the clarified butter in one or two large skillets. When it is very hot but not smoking, add the fish slices. Cook about 1 minute on one side until golden brown. Turn and cook about 1 minute on the other. Serve the fish with the sauce spooned over.

Note: Fish glaze is a long-simmered reduction of fish stock. The stock is cooked many hours until it becomes a thick, gelatinous, lightly brown mass, like thick, smooth caramel. It is a classic foundation glaze in French kitchens.

## Clarified Butter

To clarify butter, place the butter in a heatproof glass measuring cup and let it melt slowly in a 200-degree oven. Do not stir the butter. Pour off the clear, golden liquid on top, leaving the white milky substance at the bottom. The clear liquid is clarified butter.

*United States*

## Maryland Crab Cakes

*Yield: 6 crab cakes*

| | |
|---|---|
| 1 | pound backfin or lump crab meat |
| ¼ | cup finely chopped parsley |
| 1 | cup chopped scallions |
| 1¾ | cups fresh bread crumbs |
| 2 | eggs |
| ¼ | cup milk |
| | Tabasco |
| ¾ | teaspoon Worcestershire sauce |
| | Salt and freshly ground black pepper |
| 2 | tablespoons prepared mustard, preferably Dijon or Düsseldorf |
| | Oil for deep frying |
| | Tartar sauce (see recipe) |

1. If necessary, pick over the crab meat to remove any traces of shell or cartilage.

2. Empty the crab into a mixing bowl and add

the parsley, scallions, and ¾ cup of the bread crumbs.

3. In another bowl, beat the eggs and add the milk, Tabasco to taste, Worcestershire sauce, salt and pepper to taste, and mustard.

4. Blend well and pour this over the crab mixture. Stir gently to blend, leaving the crab as whole as possible. The mixture will seem rather wet and loose, but it is manageable when the cakes are finally coated with bread crumbs.

5. Shape the crab into oval or round cakes and dredge them in the remaining crumbs. Press between the hands to make the crumbs adhere and the cakes hold together.

6. Heat the oil for deep frying to 325 degrees and cook the cakes in a basket until golden brown all over. Drain and serve hot with tartar sauce.

## *Tartar Sauce*

| | |
|---|---|
| 1 | cup mayonnaise, preferably homemade |
| ¼ | cup chopped pickles, preferably sour |
| 2 | tablespoons finely chopped onions |
| 1 | hard-boiled egg, chopped |
| 1 | tablespoon finely chopped parsley |
| | Salt and freshly ground black pepper to taste |
| | Lemon juice to taste, optional |

Combine all ingredients in a mixing bowl and blend with a fork. Refrigerate until ready to use.

## *United States*

## Home-Cured Corned Beef

*Yield: 12 or more servings*

### *To Cure*

| | |
|---|---|
| 7 | quarts water |
| 3 | cups kosher salt, approximately |
| 1 | raw egg in the shell for testing brine |
| 1 | 6—9-pound brisket of beef |
| 3 | cloves garlic, peeled |
| 20 | cloves |

| 20 | black peppercorns |
| 1 | bay leaf |
| 6 | sprigs fresh thyme or 1 teaspoon dried |
| ½ | tablespoon saltpeter (available in drug stores) |

## To Cook

|  | Water to cover to a depth of 1 inch over the meat |
| 1 | bay leaf |
| 1 | onion, sliced |
| 6 | sprigs fresh thyme or 1 teaspoon dried |
| 16 | black peppercorns |
| 1 | clove garlic, sliced |
| 1 | carrot, scraped and cut into 3-inch lengths |
| 2 | ribs celery, trimmed and cut into 3-inch lengths |

1. To cure the brisket, you will need a large earthenware, enamel, or stainless-steel crock. Do not add the meat to the crock at this time.

2. Pour the water into the crock and add the salt, stirring to dissolve it. Add the egg. The egg is used to test the salt content of the brine. If the egg floats in the solution, it is ready. If it does not float, continue adding salt a little at a time, stirring to dissolve, until the egg floats. Remove the egg.

3. Add the brisket to the brine. Add the garlic, cloves, peppercorns, bay leaf, thyme, and saltpeter. Stir well. Place a clean, heavy weight on the meat to make certain it is covered. Place a lid on the crock and refrigerate for from 8 to 12 days. Turn the brisket occasionally, but keep it weighted down.

4. When ready to cook the corned beef, remove it from the brine and rinse it well.

5. Combine all the cooking ingredients in a kettle. Do not add salt. Bring to the boil and simmer 2 to 3 hours or until tender.

6. Remove the corned beef and cut it into the thinnest possible slices. Serve with rye bread slices and mustard and/or butter. Serve with garlic pickles on the side.

*Scandinavia*

## Roast Suckling Pig

*Yield: 8 to 12 servings*

| | |
|---|---|
| 1 | 10—15-pound pig |
| 1 | tablespoon salt |
| 1 | teaspoon freshly ground black pepper |
| ¾ | teaspoon dried thyme |
| | Fruit-almond stuffing (see recipe) |
| 2 | teaspoons dry mustard |
| 3 | tablespoons water |
| 1 | small apple |
| | Cranberries or cherries |
| | Parsley |

1. Preheat oven to 350 degrees.

2. Wash the pig thoroughly under cold running water and dry inside and out with paper towels. Mix the salt, pepper, and thyme and rub the mixture over the inside of the pig. Fill the cavity with the stuffing and run skewers through both sides of opening, lacing it with strings to close.

Place a raw potato or a tightly packed ball of aluminum foil the size of an apple in the pig's mouth. Cover the ears with small pieces of brown paper.

3. Place a piece of heavy-duty foil about 12 inches longer than the pig on a rack placed diagonally in an open roasting pan. Place the pig on the foil with the back legs forward. Turn the foil up loosely around the pig.

4. Place in the oven and roast 3½ to 4 hours, or about 18 minutes per pound. About 15 minutes before the pig is done, mix the mustard with 3 tablespoons water and brush over the skin.

5. Transfer the pig to a hot platter and remove the skewers, lacings, and covering on the ears. Replace the foil in the mouth with a small apple. Place cranberries or cherries in the eyes and parsley in or around the ears.

6. Pour the drippings in the foil into a saucepan and skim off the fat. Reheat and serve as a sauce.

7. For carving purposes, place the platter before the host with the head to his left.

Note: The pig's bones should separate easily at the joints. There is more meat on the shoulders than on the hind legs. Cut along the backbone to remove the chops.

## Fruit-Almond Stuffing

| | |
|---|---|
| 1 | pound almonds |
| 1½ | pounds prunes |
| 10 | large apples |
| ¼ | cup butter |
| | Salt and freshly ground black pepper |

1. Drop the almonds in boiling water and let stand until the skins slip easily. Drain, remove the skins and shred the almonds lengthwise.

2. Cook the prunes in water to cover until just tender. Drain and pit.

3. Peel, core, and slice the apples. Cook in the butter over moderately high heat until half tender. Mix the apples, almonds, prunes, salt, and pepper.

*France*

## Petits Pois à la Française
(*Stewed peas*)

*Yield: 6 servings*

| | |
|---|---|
| 1 | 6-ounce piece cured pork or slab bacon, cut into ½-inch slices and then into ½-inch-wide strips |
| 2 | dozen small white onions |
| 1 | tablespoon flour |
| 1½ | cups water |
| 2 | dozen baby carrots, peeled, or 1½ cups julienne carrots |
| 1½ | teaspoons salt |
| ¼ | teaspoon freshly ground black pepper |
| 1 | teaspoon sugar |
| 1½ | pounds fresh peas, shelled, or 1 10-ounce package frozen petit pois (small, young peas) |

1. Place the pieces of pork or bacon in a saucepan, cover with cold water, bring to a boil, and boil 1 minute. Cool under running water and drain. Pat dry.

2. Place pieces in a heavy casserole and cook over medium heat 8 minutes or until they have rendered all their fat and are well browned.

3. Add the onions and cook 1 minute. Mix in the flour, stir in the water and bring to a boil, stirring. Add the carrots, cover tightly and cook 15 minutes or until the onions and carrots are tender.

4. Add salt, pepper, sugar, and peas, bring to a boil, cover and cook 15 minutes if peas are fresh, 5 minutes if they are frozen.

*United States*

## **Rutabaga and Sweet-Potato Casserole**

*Yield: 4 to 6 servings*

| | |
|---|---|
| 2 | pounds rutabaga (yellow turnips) |
| 3/4 | pound sweet potatoes or carrots |
| | Salt |
| 3 | tablespoons butter, at room temperature |
| | Freshly ground black pepper |
| 1/4 | teaspoon grated nutmeg |
| 1/3 | cup heavy cream |

1. Preheat oven to 350 degrees.

2. Peel the rutabaga and sweet potatoes. Cut both in half, then into 2-inch chunks. If carrots are used, cut them into 2-inch lengths.

3. Place the rutabaga in a saucepan and the potatoes in another. Cover both with cold water and add salt. Bring to the boil and cook for 20 minutes or until tender. The potatoes will require less cooking than the rutabaga. Drain well.

4. While hot, put the vegetables through a food mill into a mixing bowl. Stir in 2 tablespoons butter, salt and pepper to taste, nutmeg and cream.

5. Spoon the mixture into a baking dish. Dot with remaining butter and bake 20 minutes. At the last minute place the dish under the broiler for a short time to glaze.

# Vichy Carrots

*Yield: 6 servings*

1½   pounds carrots, trimmed and scraped
    Salt and freshly ground black pepper
1   teaspoon sugar
¼   cup water or Vichy water if you want to
    be authentic
4   tablespoons butter
    Chopped parsley

1. Cut the carrots into very thin rounds. There should be about 4 cups. Put them in a skillet and add salt, pepper, sugar, water, and butter.

2. Cover with a round of buttered wax paper and cook over moderately high heat, shaking the skillet occasionally. Cook about 10 minutes, until carrots are tender, the liquid has disappeared, and they are lightly glazed. Take care they do not burn. Serve sprinkled with chopped parsley.

*France*

# Concombres Persillés

(*Parsleyed cucumbers*)

*Yield: 8 servings*

4   medium-sized cucumbers, about
    ½ pound each
    Salt
2   tablespoons butter
    Finely chopped parsley for garnish

1. Trim off and discard the ends of the cucumbers and cut the cucumbers in half widthwise. Cut each half into quarters lengthwise.

2. Using a paring knife, pare away the skin and cut away most of the center seeds but leave some of the soft center pulp.

3. Drop the cucumber pieces into boiling salted water and cook about 5 minutes. Drain and run under cold running water until chilled. Drain well.

4. Heat the butter in a skillet and add the cucumbers. Add salt and pepper to taste. Toss until thoroughly heated and serve sprinkled with chopped parsley.

*British Isles*

## Brussels Sprouts in Cream

*Yield: 6 to 8 servings*

2   10-ounce packages fresh Brussels sprouts
     Salt
3   tablespoons butter
3   tablespoons flour
1   cup cream or milk
1   egg yolk
2   tablespoons grated Parmesan cheese,
     or less to taste

1. Preheat oven to 375 degrees.

2. Pull off and discard any tough outer leaves from the sprouts. Trim the bottom of the sprouts and make a shallow incision in the form of a cross on the stem end. Place the sprouts in a skillet and add cold water to cover and salt to taste. Bring to the boil and simmer 10 to 15 minutes or until the sprouts are crisp-tender. Drain.

3. Melt 2 tablespoons of butter in a saucepan and add the flour, stirring with a whisk. When blended and smooth, add the cream, stirring vigorously with the whisk. When thickened and smooth, remove from the heat and add the egg yolk, stirring. Add salt to taste.

4. Select a casserole large enough to hold the sprouts in one layer. Melt the remaining tablespoon of butter in the casserole and add the sprouts. Carefully spoon the sauce over each sprout until they are all coated. Sprinkle with cheese and bake 10 to 12 minutes. Run the dish under the broiler briefly until nicely glazed. Serve with roast fowl.

## **Bangan Bartha**

*(Very spicy eggplant)*

Yield: 4 to 8 servings

2    eggplants, about 1 pound each or
     slightly less
8    tablespoons butter
2    cups finely chopped onion
     Salt
1    cup ripe tomatoes, cored and cut into
     thin wedges
½    cup fresh ginger, cut into small cubes or
     thin sticks the size of matchsticks
¾    cup sliced hot green peppers or use hot
     red pepper flakes to taste
1    teaspoon sweet paprika
3    tablespoons chopped fresh coriander leaves,
     optional (see note)

1. Place the eggplants on a hot charcoal grill or
loosely wrap them in heavy-duty aluminum foil
and bake in a very hot (500-degree) oven about
20 minutes. If the eggplants are to be grilled, turn
them often over the hot coals. Cook until the
eggplants are thoroughly tender throughout. Remove and let stand until cool enough to handle.

2. Melt the butter in a saucepan.

3. When the eggplants are cool, pull away the
skin, scraping off and saving the tender inside
pulp. Scoop the tender pulp into the saucepan
with the butter. Discard the skins.

4. Add the onion to the eggplant and cook 10
minutes, stirring often and taking care that the
mixture does not stick to the bottom and burn.

5. Add salt to taste and the tomatoes. Add the
ginger, peppers, and paprika and cook, stirring
often while scraping the bottom to prevent
scorching. Cook about 15 minutes and remove
from the heat. Add the chopped coriander.
Serve hot, lukewarm, or at room temperature,
with curried chicken or lamb.

Note: Fresh coriander leaves, which are also
known as cilantro and culantro in Spanish, are
available in Chinese, Spanish, Mexican, and
Italian markets.

## Pommes Pailles

*(Straw potatoes)*

Yield: 8 servings

4    large Idaho potatoes (about 1½ pounds)
     Oil for deep frying
     Salt

1. Peel the potatoes and drop them in cold water to cover.

2. Cut the potatoes into about ⅛-inch-thick slices with a knife or potato slicer. Stack the slices, a few at a time, and cut the potatoes into julienne about ⅛ inch thick. Drop the sticks into cold water as they are prepared.

3. Drain the potatoes well into a colander and dry them thoroughly.

4. Heat the oil to about 360 degrees in a cooker for deep frying. Add the potatoes, a few handfuls at a time, and cook them, stirring frequently, until they are crisp and golden brown. Drain on absorbent toweling and sprinkle with salt.

*Italy*

## Pomodori Griglia con Rosemarino

*(Grilled tomatoes with rosemary)*

Yield: 10 servings, half a tomato each

5    large, red, ripe tomatoes
1    tablespoon plus 10 teaspoons peanut,
     vegetable, or corn oil
5    teaspoons chopped fresh or dried
     rosemary leaves
     Salt and freshly ground black pepper

1. Preheat the broiler.

2. Core the tomatoes and slice them in half.

3. Grease a baking dish large enough to hold the tomato halves with 1 tablespoon of oil. Arrange the halves over it, cut side up.

4. Sprinkle each half with about ½ teaspoon of chopped rosemary, salt, and pepper. Sprinkle about 1 teaspoon oil over each half and place them under the broiler. Broil about 5 minutes.

*Germany*

## Sauerkraut

*Yield: Enough for about 18 quarts*

50  pounds white cabbage
1  pound pure granulated salt (noniodized)

1. Remove and discard the outer leaves and any other bruised or otherwise blemished leaves of the cabbage.

2. Cut the cabbage into halves, then into quarters. Cut away the white tough center cores.

3. Using a shredder or sharp slicer, cut the cabbage into fine shreds about the thickness of a penny.

4. In a kettle combine 5 pounds of the shreds with three tablespoons of salt. Blend well and let stand 15 minutes or so, until the cabbage wilts and gives up part of its liquid. Transfer this to a large sterilized crock. Add alternate layers of cabbage and salt, pressing down gently but firmly after each layer is added until juice comes to the surface. Continue until the crock is filled to within 3 or 4 inches of the top.

5. Cover the cabbage with a clean white cloth such as a double layer of cheesecloth, tucking in the sides against the inside of the container. Add a free-floating lid that will fit inside the crock and rest on the cabbage. Failing this (perhaps even preferably), add a clean, heavy plastic bag containing water to rest on the top of the cabbage. Whatever method is used, the lid or covering should extend over the cabbage to prevent exposure to the air. Air will cause the growth of film yeast or molds. The lid will also act as a weight and should offer enough weight to keep the fermenting cabbage covered with brine. Store the crock at room temperature. The ideal temperature is from 68 to 72 degrees.

6. When fermentation occurs, gas bubbles will be visible in the crock. Total time of fermentation is approximately 5 to 6 weeks.

### *How to Preserve Fresh Sauerkraut*

When the sauerkraut has fermented sufficiently, empty it into a large kettle and bring it just to the simmer. Do not boil. The correct simmering temperature is from 185 to 210 degrees. Remove the sauerkraut from the heat and pack it into hot sterilized jars. Cover with hot juice to about ½ inch from the top of the rim. Close and seal the jars with a lid and screw top. Put in a water bath and boil pint jars for 15 minutes, quart jars for 20 minutes. The sauerkraut is now ready to be stored. It will keep on the shelf for months.

Note: Sauerkraut is delicious with any kind of pork—roasts, sausages, spareribs.

*France*

## Salade des Homards
*(Lobster salad)*

*Yield: 10 servings*

- 4 cups cold, fresh, diced lobster meat (part of this may include the red coral) plus 1 cup cold, sliced lobster tails, for garnish (about 5 1½-pound lobsters in all)
- 2 hard-cooked eggs, put through a sieve
- 3 tablespoons finely chopped shallots
- 1 tablespoon chopped fresh tarragon or 1½ teaspoons dried
- 1 tablespoon chopped chives
- ¼ teaspoon chopped fresh or dried thyme
- 1 teaspoon finely minced garlic
- 2 tablespoons finely chopped parsley
- 3 tablespoons finely or coarsely chopped onion
- 2 cups mayonnaise, preferably homemade
  Lemon juice or wine vinegar
  Hard-boiled eggs, quartered, for garnish
  Tomato wedges, for garnish

Combine all the ingredients, except sliced lobster tails, quartered hard-boiled eggs, and tomato wedges, in a large mixing bowl. Add lemon juice to taste. Blend well with a rubber spatula or kitchen spoon. Serve in a bowl or in the empty body cavity of 1 very large lobster or several small. Serve garnished with the sliced lobster tails, empty claws, hard-boiled eggs, sprigs of parsley, and tomato wedges.

# **Salad Dressing à la Springs**

*Yield: About ½ cup, enough for 6*

- 2 teaspoons imported mustard, preferably Dijon or Düsseldorf
- 2 teaspoons red wine vinegar
- 2 teaspoons raw egg yolk (break the yolk and measure it)
- ¼ teaspoon Worcestershire
  Tabasco
- 6 tablespoons peanut or olive oil
  Salt and freshly ground black pepper
- 2 teaspoons heavy cream

1. Place the mustard, vinegar, egg yolk, Worcestershire sauce, and Tabasco to taste in a salad bowl.

2. Use a wire whisk and start beating the mixture rapidly. Gradually add the oil, beating constantly. The mixture should be like a thin mayonnaise. Add salt and pepper to taste and the cream. If you wish a thinner dressing, beat in a little water. And if desired, add a little fresh lemon juice to taste.

Variations: Add about ½ teaspoon finely chopped garlic and/or 1 teaspoon or more finely chopped parsley, basil, or chives, or combination of all three. Add ½ teaspoon finely chopped fresh thyme leaves.

# Cucumber Salad

*Yield: 4 servings*

2   firm, fresh, unblemished cucumbers
    Salt and freshly ground black pepper
1   tablespoon white vinegar
3   tablespoons peanut, vegetable, or corn oil
    Chopped parsley for garnish

1. Use a swivel-bladed paring knife and peel the cucumbers. Split each cucumber in half. Using a metal ball cutter or a spoon, scoop out the cucumber seeds.

2. Slice each half and put in a mixing bowl. Sprinkle lightly with salt, cover and chill at least half an hour.

3. Line a mixing bowl with cheesecloth and pour the cucumbers into it. Squeeze lightly but firmly to extract much of the liquid. Turn them into another bowl and sprinkle with salt and pepper. Add the oil and vinegar and toss. Put in a serving dish and serve sprinkled with chopped parsley as a garnish.

*France*

## Salade Niçoise
*(Tuna, anchovy and olive-based salad)*

*Yield: 6 to 8 servings*

| | |
|---|---|
| 2 | teaspoons imported mustard, preferably Dijon or Düsseldorf |
| 2 | tablespoons wine vinegar |
| 1½ | teaspoons salt |
| 1 | or 2 cloves garlic, finely minced |
| 6 | tablespoons peanut or vegetable oil |
| 6 | tablespoons olive oil |
| | Freshly ground black pepper |
| 1 | teaspoon chopped fresh thyme or ½ teaspoon dried |
| 2 | pounds green beans |
| 2 | green peppers |
| 4 | ribs celery, approximately |
| 1 | pint cherry tomatoes |
| 5 | medium, red-skinned potatoes, cooked, peeled, and sliced |
| 3 | 7-ounce cans tuna |
| 1 | 2-ounce can flat anchovies |
| 10 | stuffed olives |
| 10 | black olives, preferably imported Greek or Italian |
| 2 | small or 1 large red onion, if available, or use Bermuda onions |
| 2 | tablespoons chopped fresh basil or 1 teaspoon dried |
| ⅓ | cup finely chopped fresh parsley |
| ¼ | cup finely chopped scallions |
| 6 | hard-boiled eggs, quartered |

1. In a mixing bowl, combine the mustard, vinegar, salt, garlic, peanut oil, olive oil, pepper to taste, and thyme. Beat with a fork until well blended and set aside.

2. Pick over the beans and break them into 1½-inch lengths. Place in a saucepan and simmer in salted water to cover until tender but crisp. Drain and run under cold water, then drain in a colander and set aside.

3. Remove the cores, seeds, and white membranes from the green peppers. Cut the peppers crosswise into thin rounds and set aside.

4. Trim the celery ribs and cut crosswise into thin slices. There should be about 2 cups of sliced celery. Set aside.

5. Bring a quart of water to a boil. Drop in the cherry tomatoes and let stand for exactly 15 seconds, no longer, or they will become mushy. Drain immediately. Using a paring knife, pull off the tomato skins. Set the tomatoes aside.

6. In a large salad bowl, make a more or less symmetrical pattern of the green beans, peppers, celery, tomatoes, and potatoes. Flake the tuna and add to the bowl. Arrange the anchovies on top and scatter the olives over all.

7. Peel the onions and cut into thin, almost transparent slices. Scatter the onion rings over all. Sprinkle with basil, parsley, and scallions. Garnish with hard-boiled eggs.

8. Toss the salad with the dressing after the garnished bowl has been presented to the guests for their enjoyment. Serve with a crusty loaf of French or Italian bread.

*Germany*

## Heissen Kartoffel
## Salat mit Weisswein

*(Hot potato salad with white wine )*

*Yield: 8 cups*

Note: This recipe produces about 8 cups. To
prepare half that amount, simply divide all ingredient amounts in half.

2½ pounds potatoes
Salt and freshly ground black pepper
to taste
⅓ cup dry white wine
½ cup peanut, vegetable, or corn oil
(or olive oil if you prefer)

1. Rinse the potatoes and put them in a large
saucepan with cold water to cover. Bring to the
boil and simmer until tender, 20 minutes or
longer, depending on size. Do not cook until
mushy.

2. Preheat oven to 200 degrees.

3. Drain the potatoes and when they are cool
enough to handle, peel them. Cut them into
¼-inch-thick slices and put into a heatproof
mixing bowl. Sprinkle with salt, pepper, wine,
and oil. Toss while warm. Cover the bowl with
foil and put in the oven briefly to warm through.
Turn into a serving dish and serve while warm.

*Middle East*

## Tabbouleh
*(Syrian cracked wheat salad)*

*Yield: 6 servings*

| | |
|---|---|
| 1 | cup cracked wheat |
| ¾ | cup finely chopped onion |
| ½ | cup finely chopped scallion, green part and all |
| 1 | teaspoon salt |
| ¼ | teaspoon ground allspice |
| ¼ | teaspoon ground sumac optional (see note) |
| ¼ | teaspoon freshly ground black pepper |
| 1½ | cups finely chopped Italian parsley |
| ½ | cup finely chopped fresh mint leaves |
| ½ | cup lemon juice |
| ¾ | cup olive oil |
| 2 | tomatoes, skinned and cut into wedges or chopped |

1. Cover the cracked wheat with cold water and let stand for about 1 hour. Drain and squeeze out the extra water by hand or in a towel.

2. Add the remaining ingredients except the tomatoes and mix well. Pile into a dish and garnish with the tomatoes.

Note: This sumac, obviously not the poisonous variety, is available from Middle Eastern food stores, and spice shops.

*Italy*

## Ragu Abruzzese
*(Meat and tomato sauce for pasta)*

*Yield: About 3 quarts of sauce*

| | |
|---|---|
| 1 | cup vegetable oil |
| 2½ | pounds veal and beef bones, preferably a few marrow bones included |
| | Salt and freshly ground black pepper |
| 2¼ | pounds flank steak, cut into ½-inch-thick rectangles, measuring about 2 by 4 inches |
| ½ | pound butter |
| ¾ | cup finely chopped heart of celery |
| 1½ | cups chopped onion |
| ½ | cup chopped shallots |
| 3 | cloves garlic, chopped |
| 3 | bay leaves |
| 2 | cups dry red wine |
| 4 | quarts tomatoes, put through a sieve or food mill to eliminate seeds |
| 1 | cup tomato paste |
| 1½ | cups water |
| 1 | sprig fresh rosemary or 1 tablespoon dried, tied in a cheesecloth bag |
| ¾ | cup dried Italian mushrooms |

1. Heat the oil in a heavy kettle and add the bones. Sprinkle with salt and pepper and cook, stirring occasionally, until nicely browned, about 10 or 15 minutes.

2. Add the meat and cook, stirring occasionally, about 30 minutes or until browned. Pour off fat from kettle.

3. Add the butter, celery, onion, shallots, garlic, and bay leaves. Cook about 20 minutes, stirring occasionally. Add the wine and simmer 10 minutes. Add the tomatoes, tomato paste, and water. Cook about 30 minutes and add the rosemary.

4. Cook about 1 hour longer. Remove the bones.

The meat clinging to the bones is excellent for nibbling on.

5. Remove and discard the bay leaves and cheesecloth bag.

6. Cover the mushrooms with water and bring to the boil. Simmer about 1 minute. Drain and add to the tomato sauce. Cook briefly. This sauce is now ready to be served with almost any form of pasta. The meat may be served with the sauce or separately after the pasta course. This sauce will keep for several days in the refrigerator and much longer if reheated occasionally. It freezes well.

*France*

## Basic Chicken Broth

*Yield: About 5 cups*

| | |
|---|---|
| 3 | pounds bony chicken parts such as wings, necks, and backs |
| 1 | bay leaf |
| $\frac{1}{2}$ | teaspoon dried thyme |
| 12 | black peppercorns |
| 2 | ribs celery with leaves |
| 1 | large onion, peeled and studded with 2 cloves |
| 1 | carrot, scraped and coarsely chopped |
| 6 | sprigs parsley |
| 10 | cups water |
| 1 | tablespoon salt |

1. Place the chicken pieces in a large saucepan or kettle. Add the remaining ingredients and bring to a boil over moderate heat. Simmer, uncovered, for 2 hours. Using a large kitchen spoon, skim from time to time all the scum and foam that rises to the top of the soup as it boils, rinsing the spoon occasionally between skimmings.

2. Place a sieve over a large mixing bowl and line it with a piece of cheesecloth that has been rinsed in cold water. Very carefully pour the soup into the sieve so that it is strained into the bowl. Discard all the solid matter such as the bones, skin, meat, vegetables, and spices.

## Basic Fish Stock

*Yield: About 6 cups*

2   pounds bones from a white-fleshed, nonoily fish, including heads if possible

6   cups water

1   cup dry white wine

1   cup coarsely chopped celery

1   cup coarsely chopped onion

3   sprigs fresh thyme or 1 teaspoon dried

1   bay leaf

10   black peppercorns

    Salt

1   medium-size tomato, cored, optional

1. If the fish heads are used, the gills must be removed. Run the bones under cold running water.

2. Place the bones in a kettle or deep saucepan and add the remaining ingredients. Bring to the boil and simmer 20 minutes. Strain.

Note: Leftover stock can be frozen for use in other dishes.

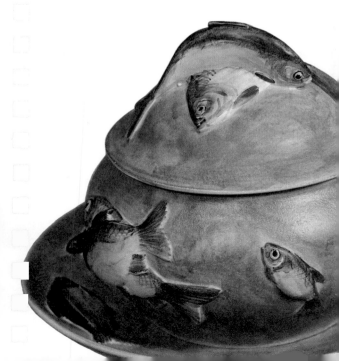

*France*

## Mustard Hollandaise

*Yield: 6 or more servings*

| | |
|---|---|
| 3 | tablespoons dry mustard |
| 1/4 | teaspoon salt |
| 1/2 | teaspoon sugar |
| 2 | tablespoons water |
| 1/2 | pound butter |
| 2 | egg yolks |
| 1 | tablespoon water |
| 1 | tablespoon lemon juice |

1. Place the mustard in a small bowl and add salt, sugar and water. Mix and let stand at least 10 minutes to develop flavor.

2. Preheat the oven to 200 degrees.

3. Place the butter in a 1-quart glass measuring cup (this will facilitate pouring the butter later) and set it carefully in the oven to melt.

4. When the butter is melted, carefully remove the measuring cup, using a pot holder. Turn off the oven heat. Using a heavy kitchen spoon, or small ladle, skim off the foam and scum from the top of the butter. Carefully pour off the clear golden liquid. Discard the white milky substance in the bottom. There should be about 3/4 cup of clear, liquid butter.

5. In a heavy saucepan, combine the egg yolks with the water. Place the saucepan over a Flame-Tamer or asbestos pad and start whisking the yolks rapidly with the water. Whisk thoroughly until the mixture becomes thick and foamy like a custard, about 5 to 10 minutes. Do not let the mixture become too hot or it will break down and curdle. Remove the saucepan from the heat and, beating vigorously, gradually add the melted butter. Add the lemon juice. Stir in the mustard according to taste.

# Aïoli
*(Garlic mayonnaise)*

*Yield: About 2 cups of aïoli*

3 egg yolks
Salt
Freshly ground black pepper
1 tablespoon prepared mustard, preferably Dijon or Düsseldorf
1 tablespoon finely minced garlic, or more according to taste
1 tablespoon white wine vinegar
2 cups olive oil
Tabasco to taste

1. Place the yolks in a mixing bowl and add salt, pepper, mustard, garlic, and vinegar.

2. Start beating with a wire whisk or an electric blender and gradually add the oil. When the mixture starts to thicken, the oil may be added in ever increasing quantities. Continue beating until all the oil is used. Add the Tabasco. If a thinner mayonnaise is desired, beat in a teaspoon of cold water.

Note: Aïoli is the name not only of this Provençal garlic sauce but of the assortment of dishes that accompany it. Traditionally, this assortment consists of salt cod, which has been soaked, then simmered in water with cloves until cooked, and artichokes, carrots, cauliflower, potatoes, chick peas, and eggs—all cooked separately but served together on a large platter. The sauce, of course, can be served with any one dish alone.

*Austria*

## Spanische Windtorte
*(Baked meringue with whipped cream
    and strawberries)*

| | |
|---|---|
| 12 | egg whites at room temperature |
| 1/8 | teaspoon salt |
| 3/4 | teaspoon cream of tartar |
| 3 | cups superfine sugar, sieved |
| | Parchment paper or unglazed brown paper |
| 4 | cups heavy cream, whipped |
| 3 | tablespoons confectioners' sugar |
| 1 | quart strawberries |

1. Preheat the oven to 150 to 200 degrees.

2. Place sheets of parchment paper on slightly damp baking sheets and mark off 5 8-inch circles.

3. Place 8 of the egg whites in a large electric mixer bowl. Add half the salt. Beat until frothy, then add ½ teaspoon of the cream of tartar. (The whites can also be beaten in a copper bowl with a balloon whisk.)

4. Continue to beat and gradually add, a tablespoon at a time, 1¾ cups of the superfine sugar. Beat until the mixture is smooth and glossy and there is no hint of graininess when the mixture is felt between the fingers.

5. Fold in ¼ cup more of the superfine sugar and transfer the mixture to a large piping bag fitted with a no. 8 plain tube.

6. Starting in the center of the first circle, make a snail-like pattern, going around and around until the edge of the circle is covered. This will be the bottom layer of the cake.

7. On the next 3 circles, make a ring of piped

meringue, 2 layers high, around the outside edge. These will form the sides of the cake.

8. On the last circle, using a no. 6 star tube this time, pipe the meringue into a fairly thick, single-layer ring around the edge. Fill in the center with crisscrossed lattice work substantial enough to enable this layer to be lifted off and used for the top of the cake.

9. Bake, or rather dry, all 5 circles of meringue for 2 to 3 hours, or until they are crisp but have not taken on any color. When they are dry, they will be easily removable from the parchment paper if care is taken.

10. Beat the remaining 4 egg whites, with the remaining salt, until frothy. Add the remaining ¼ teaspoon cream of tartar and beat until peaks form.

11. Gradually, a tablespoon at a time, beat in ¾ cup of the remaining superfine sugar. Beat until the mixture is smooth and glossy and does not feel grainy. Fold in the remaining ¼ cup superfine sugar.

12. Place the solid circle on a serving plate. Dot around the edges with meringue and put the first ring in place. Dot the top of this ring and position the second ring. Repeat with the third ring.

13. With a spatula, use meringue to frost all around the outside of the cake shell to make a smooth surface. Transfer the remaining meringue to a piping bag fitted with a no. 6 star tube and decorate the cake around the bottom and on the sides. Bake, or dry, at 200 degrees, or below, several hours or overnight.

14. To serve, combine the whipped cream with the confectioners' sugar and strawberries, sliced except for a few left whole for garnish. Pile into the cake shell. Top with the lattice meringue top and garnish with the whole strawberries.

Note: For best results this dessert should not be attempted on a damp or humid day. If baked meringue breaks, it can be mended by "gluing" it together with unbaked meringue.

# Irish Whiskey Pie

*Yield: 8 or more servings*

## Crust

1¼   cups graham cracker crumbs
¼   cup sugar
½   cup melted butter

## Filling

½   cup cold strong coffee
1   envelope unflavored gelatin
⅔   cup sugar
    Salt
3   eggs, separated
6   tablespoons Irish whiskey
¼   cup coffee liqueur
2   cups heavy cream

1. Preheat the oven to 350 degrees.

2. To make the crust, combine the crumbs with the sugar and melted butter and rub together until the crumbs are evenly coated. Spoon the crumbs into a 9- or 10-inch pie plate and press the crumbs evenly against the bottom and sides.

3. Bake pie shell 4 to 5 minutes without browning. Remove from heat, cool thoroughly.

4. To make filling, pour the coffee into a saucepan and sprinkle gelatin over it. Add half the sugar, salt, and yolks. Blend thoroughly.

5. Place the saucepan over low heat and stir until the gelatin is dissolved and the mixture thickens. Do not boil.

6. Remove the mixture from the heat and add the Irish whiskey and coffee liqueur. Chill the mixture in the refrigerator until it is cool and starts to thicken. Do not let it jell.

7. Beat the whites until stiff, gradually adding the remaining sugar. Fold this into the gelatin.

8. Whip 1 cup of heavy cream and fold it into the mixture. Turn this into the prepared pie plate and chill several hours or overnight.

9. Before serving, whip the remaining cream, adding sugar to taste. Garnish with whipped cream and serve.

*France*

## Frozen Lemon Soufflé

*Yield: 8 servings*

- 12   egg yolks
- 1¾   cups plus 2 teaspoons sugar
- ¾   cup lemon juice (from approximately 4 lemons)
-     Grated rind of 1 lemon
- ½   cup heavy cream
- 6   egg whites
-     Whipped cream for garnish, optional
-     Candied flowers for garnish, optional

1. Select a skillet with deep sides into which a 2-quart bowl will fit comfortably. Add enough water to come up around the sides of the bowl without overflowing. Remove the bowl and start heating water in skillet.

2. Drop yolks and 1½ cups of sugar into bowl and beat with a whisk or portable electric mixer until light and lemon colored. Add the lemon juice and, when water is boiling, set the bowl in the skillet and continue beating about 10 minutes or until the egg mixture is like a very thick, smooth, and creamy custard. The temperature of the egg mixture at this point should be 120 to 140 degrees.

3. Scrape the mixture into another mixing bowl and stir in the lemon rind. Let cool and chill thoroughly on ice or in refrigerator.

4. Prepare a 5-cup soufflé dish. Tear off a length of wax paper that will fit around the outside of the soufflé dish, adding 1 or 2 inches for overlap.

5. Fold the wax paper lengthwise into thirds. Wrap it around the outside of the soufflé dish about 2 inches above the rim, making sure that it overlaps itself at the ends by at least 1 inch. Secure it with string or paper clips.

6. Beat the ½ cup of heavy cream and when it starts to thicken, add 2 teaspoons sugar. Continue beating until stiff. Fold this into the egg mixture.

7. In a separate bowl beat the whites. When they start to mound, add the remaining ¼ cup of sugar, beating constantly. Continue beating until whites are stiff. Fold them into the soufflé mixture.

8. Pour the mixture into the prepared dish and place in the freezer. Let stand several hours—or overnight—until frozen.

9. Remove the wax paper. Decorate if desired with whipped cream, piped out of a pastry tube, and candied flowers.

*Barbados*

## Rum Ice Cream

*Yield: About 24 servings*

| | |
|---|---|
| 10 | egg yolks |
| 1½ | cups sugar |
| 4 | cups milk |
| 4 | cups heavy cream |
| ¾ | cup rum |

1. Place the yolks in a large saucepan and add the sugar. Beat with whisk until thick and lemon colored.

2. Meanwhile, bring the milk and cream almost but not quite to the boil.

3. Gradually add the milk and cream to the yolk mixture, beating constantly. Use a wooden spoon and stir constantly, this way and that, making certain that the spoon touches all over the bottom of the saucepan. If a thermometer is available, use it. Cook to 180 degrees and remove the saucepan from the heat. If a thermometer is not available, cook the sauce until it becomes like a very thin custard. Continue stirring briefly after the sauce has been removed from the heat. Cool and chill.

4. Pour the sauce into the container of an electric or hand-cranked ice-cream freezer. Add the rum. Freeze according to the manufacturer's instructions. Serve, if desired, with a little additional spirit poured over each serving.

## **Christmas Stollen**
*(Fruit, nut and spice-filled loaf)*

Yield: 1 stollen

| | |
|---|---|
| ⅔ | cup milk, scalded |
| ⅔ | cup sugar |
| ¾ | teaspoon salt |
| | Butter |
| 2 | tablespoons vegetable shortening |
| 2 | packages dry yeast |
| ¼ | cup warm water |
| 2 | eggs, lightly beaten |
| ½ | teaspoon ground cinnamon |
| ⅛ | teaspoon ground mace |
| ⅛ | teaspoon ground cardamom |
| 3½ | cups sifted all-purpose flour, approximately |
| 1 | cup diced mixed candied fruits |
| ¼ | cup raisins |
| ½ | cup chopped pecans |
| | Quick Fondant Icing (see recipe, page 118) |
| | Pecan halves |

1. Pour the milk into a large bowl. Add the sugar, salt, ¼ pound butter, and shortening. Stir to melt the butter and dissolve the sugar. Let cool to lukewarm.

2. Soften the yeast in the warm water and add to the cooled mixture. Beat in the eggs, cinnamon, mace, and cardamom, and enough flour to make a soft dough that can be kneaded.

3. Turn onto a lightly floured board and knead until smooth. Knead in the fruits (first tossed in a little flour), raisins, and chopped nuts until evenly distributed.

4. Place the dough in a greased bowl. Cover and let rise in a warm place until doubled in bulk, about 2½ to 3 hours.

5. Punch down and roll into an oval about 12 by 8 inches. Fold over lengthwise so that the two edges do not quite meet.

6. Place on a greased baking sheet, cover, and let rise in a warm place until doubled in bulk, about 1½ to 2 hours.

7. Preheat the oven to 400 degrees. Bake the stollen 10 minutes. Reduce the oven tempera-

ture to 350 degrees and bake 25 minutes longer, or until the loaf sounds hollow when tapped on the bottom.

8. Brush with butter and let cool on a rack. When cool, spread with the icing and decorate with pecan halves.

*Canada*

## Fruitcake

Yield: 1 2¼-pound loaf or 6-cup tube pan and
2 3-pound cakes

| | |
|---|---|
| ½ | cup (3½ ounces) chopped glacé cherries (see note) |
| 1½ | cups (10—12 ounces) chopped glacé pineapple (see note) |
| 3 | cups (15 ounces) seedless black raisins |
| 1½ | cups (8 ounces) dried black currants |
| 2 | cups (8 ounces) broken pecans |
| 1½ | cups (8 ounces) chopped blanched almonds |
| 1 | cup bourbon, cognac, or rum |
| 2½ | cups flour |
| ½ | pound butter |
| 1¾ | cups sugar |
| 6 | eggs, separated |
| 2 | teaspoons baking powder |
| ¾ | teaspoon baking soda |
| 1½ | teaspoons ground ginger |
| 1½ | teaspoons ground mace |
| 1 | tablespoon grated nutmeg |
| 1 | tablespoon ground cinnamon |
| 1 | cup orange juice |
| 4 | cups grated fresh coconut or 2 cups unsweetened dried coconut (available in health food outlets) |
| 1 | cup (12 ounces) fig preserves |
| ½ | cup quince, apricot, or grape jelly |
| | Quick Fondant Icing (see recipe), optional |
| | Candied fruits such as cherries, angelica, and so on, for decorating the cake, optional. |

1. Combine the cherries, pineapple, raisins, currants, pecans, and almonds in a mixing bowl and add ½ cup of bourbon, cognac, or rum. Cover with plastic wrap and let stand overnight.

2. Preheat oven to 250 degrees.

3. Empty the fruits onto a flat surface and sprinkle with ½ cup of flour. Toss to coat the fruits and nuts and set aside.

4. Put the butter into the bowl of an electric mixer. Add the sugar and start beating first on low and then on high speed. Cream the mixture well until it is light colored. Beat in the egg yolks one at a time.

5. Meanwhile, combine the remaining 2 cups of flour with the baking powder, soda, ginger, mace, nutmeg and cinnamon. Sift the dry ingredients together.

6. Gradually beat the flour mixture into the butter and sugar mixture. Gradually beat in the orange juice, remaining ½ cup of bourbon, cognac, or rum, coconut, fig preserves, and quince jelly. Fold in the floured fruit.

7. Prepare the baking pans by butttering them well. Line them with a double layer of wax paper or one layer of parchment paper and grease the paper. If using Teflon-coated pans, butter the pan and line the bottom with a cutout of wax paper and butter. The batter may be portioned into pans of various sizes, but do not fill any pan full of batter, for it expands as it bakes. Always leave about 1 inch of space from the top of the pan. This recipe was most recently tested with 2 standard 9-by-5-inch Teflon loaf pans plus 1 8½-by-4½-by-3-inch (6 cup) loaf pan (a 6-cup round tube pan could also be used).

8. Beat the egg whites until they stand in stiff peaks. Fold them into the batter. This recipe yields about 4 quarts (16 cups) of batter.

9. Fill baking pans. Bake the cakes for 2½ hours and increase the heat to 275 degrees. Bake a total of about 3½ hours for the large loaf pans, a total of about 3¼ for the smaller ones. Cooking times will vary from oven to oven. The correct internal temperature for these cakes is 160 degrees when a meat thermometer is inserted.

10. When the cakes are removed from the oven, cool on a rack for at least 30 minutes, run a knife

around the edges and while still warm invert them on a rack. They should not stick to the bottom, but if they do, scrape out the stuck portion and repair the bottom with that. Frost with icing and decorate, if desired, with candied fruit.

Note: Candied fruits including glacé cherries and pineapple are available in many fine food stores. These cakes may be kept for days, weeks, and months before they are frosted. To keep them, store closely covered in a dry place. Douse them occasionally with a ¼ cup or so of bourbon, rum, or cognac.

## *Quick Fondant Icing*

*Yield: Sufficient icing for 1 fruitcake*

| | |
|---|---|
| ½ | cup granulated sugar |
| 2½ | tablespoons white corn syrup |
| ¼ | cup water |
| 1½ | cups confectioners' sugar |
| 1 | teaspoon egg white |
| 1 | teaspoon butter at room temperature |
| | Bourbon, rum, or cognac |

1. Combine the granulated sugar, corn syrup, and water in a saucepan and gradually bring to the boil, stirring until sugar is dissolved. Cook over moderate heat until mixture registers 236 to 238 degrees on a candy thermometer.

2. Have ready a pastry brush in a cup of cold water. As the syrup cooks, run the brush around the inside of the saucepan, wiping away sugar crystals that may form above the syrup. If not removed, these will cause crystals throughout the syrup. When the syrup is ready, pour it into another saucepan and let cool.

3. Place the saucepan into a skillet or larger saucepan with water. Bring the water to the boil. Stir the syrup until it is fluid.

4. Gradually add the confectioners' sugar into the syrup, stirring constantly. Stir until well blended and lukewarm. Do not overheat.

5. Beat in the egg white and butter and add enough bourbon, rum, or cognac to bring the icing to a spreadable consistency.

## Chocolate Cake

*Yield: 8 to 12 servings*

| | |
|---|---|
| 10 | eggs, separated and at room temperature or slightly warmer |
| 14 | tablespoons (about 1 cup) sugar |
| 6 | ounces bittersweet or semisweet chocolate, melted slowly over hot water and cooled |
| 2 | cups finely chopped (not ground) walnuts |

1. Preheat oven to 350 degrees.

2. Beat the egg yolks and sugar until very thick and lemon colored. Stir in the chocolate. Fold in the nuts.

3. Beat the egg whites until stiff but not dry and fold into the chocolate-nut mixture. Turn into a greased 10-inch spring form pan and bake one hour or until the center springs back when lightly touched with fingertips. Cool in pan.

*Italy*

## Marzapane
(*Almond cake*)

*Yield: 12 or more servings*

| | |
|---|---|
| 7 | egg whites |
| 3 | cups instant superfine sugar |
| 8 | cups ground almonds |
| 2 | tablespoons Arum (an Italian orange liqueur) or Grand Marnier |
| 5 | cups flour |
| 6 | sheets rice paper |

1. Preheat the oven to 350 degrees.

2. Beat the egg whites until they stand in very stiff peaks.

3. Beat in the sugar and fold in the almonds until thoroughly blended. Add the liqueur.

4. Put the flour into a standard jellyroll pan measuring about 10 by 15 inches. Smooth it over with a spatula and cover the flour neatly with 4 overlapping sheets of rice paper. Spoon the almond mixture on top and smooth it over with a spatula almost but not quite to the edge of the pan. Cover with two sheets of rice paper. Bake 15 to 20 minutes.

*United States*

## Indian Pudding

*Yield: 8 or more servings*

- 5 cups milk
- ⅔ cup yellow cornmeal
  Salt
- 1 cup finely chopped beef suet
- 1 cup molasses
- 1 cup sugar
- 1 large egg
- 1 seedless orange
- 1 cup seedless raisins
- ½ cup dried currants
- ½ teaspoon ground cinnamon
- ½ teaspoon ground allspice
- ½ teaspoon ground cloves
- ½ teaspoon grated nutmeg
- 1 teaspoon baking powder

1. Preheat oven to 300 degrees.

2. Bring 4 cups of milk just to the boil and add it to the top of a double boiler. Gradually add the cornmeal, stirring constantly with a wire whisk. Stir in salt to taste and suet. Cook, stirring, about 20 minutes.

3. Stir in the molasses, sugar, and egg.

4. Trim off the stem end of the orange. Slice the orange thinly, then cut each slice—flesh, skin, juice, and all—into very small cubes. Add the orange to the cornmeal mixture.

5. Finely chop or grind the raisins and add them. Add the currants and all the spices. Blend remaining cup of milk with baking powder and stir it in.

6. Generously butter a 2-quart crock or casserole, preferably made of stoneware. Pour in the mixture. Do not cover. Bake about 2 to 2½ hours until set. Serve warm with English Custard (see recipe) or vanilla ice cream.

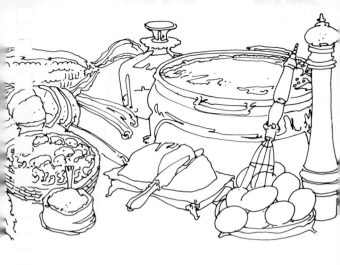

## English Custard

| | |
|---|---|
| 4 | whole eggs |
| 2 | egg yolks |
| 1/3 | cup sugar |
| 3 | cups milk |
| 1/4 | teaspoon salt |
| 1 | teaspoon vanilla |

1. Combine the eggs, egg yolks, and sugar in a saucepan. Beat with a wire whisk until thick and lemon colored.

2. Meanwhile, bring the milk almost but not quite to the boil.

3. Gradually add the milk to the yolk mixture, beating constantly, this way and that, making certain that the spoon touches all over the bottom of the saucepan. Cook, stirring, and add the salt. Cook until the mixture has a custardlike consistency and coats the sides of the spoon. Do not let the sauce boil, or it will curdle.

4. Immediately remove the sauce from the stove, but continue stirring. Add the vanilla. Set the saucepan in a basin of cold water to reduce the temperature. Let the sauce cool to room temperature. Chill.

*France*

## Tarte de Friande

*(Apple tart)*

Yield: 10 servings

Sweet Pastry Dough (see recipe)

| | |
|---|---|
| 3½ | pounds Golden Delicious apples, about 9 |
| 12 | tablespoons butter |
| 1 | 1-inch piece of vanilla bean, optional |
| ¼ | cup confectioners' sugar |
| ½ | cup marmalade |
| 2 | tablespoons water |
| 2 | tablespcons Grand Marnier |
| ¼ | cup toasted, slivered almonds |

1. Preheat oven to 400 degrees.

2. Roll out the pastry on a very cold board or surface (it will be hard to handle otherwise) and fit it into a 10-inch flan ring or pie plate. Refrigerate.

3. Peel and halve the apples. Cut away and discard the cores. Select 12 choice apple halves to be used for the top of the tart. Cut off the small ends of each of these halves (about ¼ inch on both sides). Set the 12 apple halves aside.

4. Quarter the remaining apple halves. Cut them into very thin slices. There should be about 8 cups.

5. Heat 8 tablespoons of butter in a large heavy skillet and add the thinly sliced apples. Add the piece of vanilla bean and cook about 30 minutes, stirring, until the apples are quite dry and appetizingly browned. Stir in the remaining butter.

6. Spoon the browned apple mixture into the pastry-lined flan ring and smooth it over. Thinly slice the reserved apple halves and arrange them neatly—layer after layer—in an overlapping pattern over the cooked apples.

7. Spoon the confectioners' sugar into a small sieve and sieve it evenly over the tart.

8. Bake the tart about 1 hour.

9. Combine the marmalade and water in a saucepan and stir until thinned. Let cool and add the Grand Marnier. Spread it over the tart and sprinkle the toasted almonds over all.

## Sweet Pastry Dough

*Yield: Enough pastry for a 9- or 10-inch crust*

- ¼ pound very cold butter
- ½ cup confectioners' sugar
- 2 egg yolks
- 1¼ cups flour
  Salt
- ½—1 tablespoon ice water

1. Cut the butter into small cubes and put it in a mixing bowl.

2. Add the sugar and egg yolks and mix thoroughly, using the hands or an electric beater.

3. Combine the flour and salt in a flour sifter. Sift them gradually and alternately with the water to the yolk mixture. Add just enough water so that the mixture holds together. Shape the dough into a flat cake and wrap it in wax paper. Refrigerate for ½ hour or so. Remember the pastry will work best if it is rolled out on a very cold surface, preferably marble.

## **Grand Marnier Sauce**

*Yield: 10 to 12 servings*

| | |
|---|---|
| 5 | egg yolks |
| ½ | cup plus 2 tablespoons sugar |
| ½ | cup Grand Marnier |
| 1 | cup heavy cream |

1. Select a 2-quart mixing bowl that will rest snugly on top of a slightly larger saucepan. Add about 2 inches of water to the saucepan and bring it to the boil.

2. Add the yolks and ½ cup of sugar and beat vigorously and thoroughly with a wire whisk or portable electric beater, making certain that you scrape around the inside bottom of the bowl with the beater.

3. Place the mixing bowl on the saucepan (over but not in the water) and continue beating.

4. Beat 10 minutes or so until the yolks are quite thick and pale yellow. Remove the bowl from the saucepan and stir in ½ the Grand Marnier. Let the sauce cool, then refrigerate until thoroughly cold.

5. Beat the cream with the 2 tablespoons of sugar almost but not quite to the stiff state. Fold the cream into the sauce. Stir in remaining Grand Marnier.

Note: This sauce is superb on fresh strawberries or other fruit in season or on any fruit tart.

## Coupe Normande

*(Vanilla ice cream with apples and Calvados)*

Yield: 6 servings

| | |
|---|---|
| 4 | firm cooking apples |
| 4 | tablespoons butter |
| ½ | cup sugar |
| ¼ | cup Calvados or applejack |
| 6 | servings vanilla ice cream |

1. Core and peel the apples. Cut them into quarters and cut the quarters into slices. There should be about 4 cups.

2. Heat the butter in a heavy skillet and add the apples. Cook, stirring gently and tossing, about 6 to 10 minutes. The slices should remain firm and not become mushy.

3. Add the sugar and cook 2 minutes, stirring and tossing gently.

4. Sprinkle with Calvados and ignite it. Serve hot or warm over vanilla ice cream.

*France*

## Grapefruit and Lemon Ice

Yield: 1½ quarts

| | |
|---|---|
| 2 | cups sugar |
| 2 | cups water |
| | Grated rind of 1 grapefruit |
| 4 | cups fresh, unsweetened grapefruit juice (from 4 or 5 grapefruits) |
| ⅓ | cup lemon juice (2—3 lemons) |

1. Combine the sugar and water in a saucepan and bring to the boil, stirring until sugar is dissolved. Boil 5 minutes and add the grated rind. Remove from the heat and let cool thoroughly.

2. Combine the syrup, grapefruit juice, and lemon juice in the container of an electric ice-cream maker. Freeze according to the manufacturer's instructions. Scoop the ice into a mixing bowl, packing it down. Cover with plastic wrap and place in the freezer until ready to use.

Note: This ice is delectable served with sweetened grapefruit sections steeped in a little vodka.

# **Pears in Caramel Syrup**

*Yield: 8 servings*

| | |
|---|---|
| 8 | firm, unblemished, ripe pears, preferably Comice or Anjou |
| | Juice of 1 lemon |
| 2 | cups sugar |
| ⅓ | cup coffee liqueur |
| | Whipped cream, optional |

1. Peel the pears, leaving the stems on. As each pear is peeled drop it into water with lemon juice added to prevent discoloration.

2. Measure 3 cups of water into a saucepan and add half the sugar. Bring to the boil and add the pears. Cook the pears in the liquid, turning them gently on occasion, until they are tender but firm, about 20 minutes or more. Carefully remove the pears and reserve the syrup. Arrange the pears neatly on a serving dish.

3. Pour 1 cup of the reserved syrup into a saucepan and add the remaining sugar. Bring to the boil. Cook 5 to 10 minutes until the syrup starts to caramelize, shaking the skillet in a circular fashion. When quite brown but not burned, quickly remove the saucepan from the heat and add the remaining syrup. Take care that you do not burn yourself. Bring to the boil again and add the coffee liqueur. Pour the sauce over the pears and chill. Serve cold with whipped cream if desired.

*United States*

# Mississippi Delta Eggnog

*Yield: 6 to 8 servings*

8 large eggs, separated
¾ cup sugar
1 cup bourbon or more to taste
½ cup heavy cream
  Grated nutmeg

1. Put the egg yolks and sugar into the bowl of an electric mixer and beat until light and lemon colored.

2. Gradually add the whiskey, beating on low speed.

3. Whip the cream until stiff and fold it into the egg yolk mixture.

4. Whip the egg whites until stiff peaks form and fold them into the eggnog. Serve in goblets or mugs with a sprinkling of nutmeg on top.

*United States*

# Hot Spiced Cider

*Yield: 8 servings*

2 quarts fresh apple cider
3 slices fresh lemon
2 tablespoons honey
1 2-inch piece of stick cinnamon
6 whole cloves
  A jigger of rum, optional

1. Combine all the ingredients, except the rum, in a saucepan and bring to the boil. Cover and simmer 10 minutes.

2. Strain into hot mugs. Add jigger of rum to each serving if desired.

*Mexico*

## **Margarita**

*Yield: 1 cocktail*

1½   ounces tequila
     Juice of ½ lime
 1   ounce Triple Sec or Cointreau
½   lime
     Salt

1. Fill a cocktail shaker with ice cubes and add all the above ingredients except ½ lime and salt.

2. Cover with a bar glass and shake thoroughly.

3. Rub the rim of a champagne or tulip-shaped glass with the cut half of a lime and dip the rim into salt. We use coarse kosher salt. Strain the mixture into the prepared glass and serve.

## Sicilian Cocktail

*Yield: 1 serving*

1    ounce vodka
2    ounces Campari aperitif
2    drops Angostura bitters
1    teaspoon sugar or to taste
     Lemon peel

1. Combine the vodka and Campari in a cocktail shaker. Add the bitters and sugar. Shake well with cracked ice and strain into a cocktail glass.

2. Add a twist of lemon and serve.

*Haiti*

## Rum Punch

*Yield: 6 to 8 servings*

1    6-ounce can (¾ cup) frozen pink
     lemonade, slightly defrosted
6    tablespoons (½ can) water
1    large-size pitted peach (see note)
¼    cup Triple Sec, Cointreau, Grenadine, or
     cassis syrup
1¼   cups dark Haitian rum or other dark rum

Combine all the ingredients in the container of an electric blender. Blend thoroughly. Serve in individual glasses over ice cubes.

Note: Almost any fruit may be used to replace the peach. Peeled, pitted mangoes (about ¼ mango per recipe) are excellent.

*Russia*

## Vodka with Lemon Peel

*Yield: 1 bottle of vodka*

1    lemon
1    bottle vodka

1. Peel the lemon with a potato peeler and carefully cut away any white pulp.

2. Add the yellow peel to the vodka. Seal and let stand at room temperature for 24 hours. Place in freezer several hours before serving.

# Strawberry Fizz

*Yield: 1 serving*

- ½    pint fresh strawberries
- 1½    ounces vodka (see note)
-       Juice of ½ orange
- 2    teaspoons sugar
- 1    teaspoon egg white

1. Pick over the berries and remove the stems. Rinse the berries in cold water and drain. Put the prepared berries in the container of an electric blender and blend, stirring down as necessary. This should make ½ cup of fresh juice.

2. Put the ½ cup of juice in a bar glass and add the remaining ingredients. Add cracked ice and shake well. Strain and serve.

Note: In Peru, this drink is made with a brandy called Pisco rather than vodka.

The stores listed below are reported to accept mail orders; some of them make catalogs available for that purpose. When making inquiries, find out if there is a minimum mail order charge. Mr. Claiborne suggests you order by mail only if the ingredients you need are not available in your community. In urban areas, Ethnic foods are usually not hard to find. This listing does not constitute an endorsement on our part. It is provided solely as a guide.

## CARIBBEAN, SOUTH AMERICAN, AND MEXICAN

### Colorado

American Tea, Coffee and Spice Company
1511 Champa Street
Denver 80202

### Louisiana

Central Grocery Company
923 Decatur Street
New Orleans 70116

## CHINESE

### California

Wing Chong Lung Co.
922 South San Pedro Street
Los Angeles 90015

### Illinois

Star Market
3349 North Clark Street
Chicago 60657

### New York

H. Roth and Son
1577 First Avenue
New York 10028

## INDIAN

### Colorado

American Tea, Coffee and Spice Company
1511 Champa Street
Denver 80202

### Massachusetts

Cambridge Coffee, Tea and Spice House
1765 Massachusetts Avenue
Cambridge 02140

### New York

Kalustyan Orient Export Trading Corporation
123 Lexington Avenue
New York 10016

H. Roth and Son
1577 First Avenue
New York 10028

### Texas

Antone's
Box 3352
Houston 77001

## INDONESIAN

### California
Holland American Market
10343 East Artesia Boulevard
Bellflower 90706

### Missouri
Asia Food Products
1509 Delmar Boulevard
St. Louis 63103

### New York
Toko Garuda
997 First Avenue
New York 10022

H. Roth and Son
1577 First Avenue
New York 10028

## JAPANESE

### Colorado
Pacific Mercantile Company
1946 Larimer Street
Denver 80202

### Illinois
Diamond Trading Company
1108 North Clark Street
Chicago 60610

### Kansas
Imported Foods
1038 McCormick
Wichita 67213

### Louisiana
Oriental Trading Company
2636 Edenborn Avenue
Metairie 70002

### New York
Katagiri Company
225 East 59th Street
New York 10022

H. Roth and Son
1577 First Avenue
New York 10028

### Ohio
Soya Food Products
2356 Wyoming Avenue
Cincinnati 45214

## MIDDLE EASTERN

### Massachusetts
Cardullo's Gourmet Shop
6 Brattle Street
Cambridge 02138

### Michigan
American Oriental Grocery
20736 Lahser Road
Southfield 48075

### Missouri
Demmas Shish-Ke-Bab
5806 Hampton Avenue
St. Louis 63109

### New York
Malko Brothers
197 Atlantic Avenue
Brooklyn 11201

H. Roth and Son
1577 First Avenue
New York 10028

## VIETNAMESE

### Virginia
Viet Nam Center, Inc.
3133 Wilson Boulevard
Arlington 22201

## KITCHENWARE

### New York
The Bridge Kitchenware Corporation
212 East 52nd Street
New York 10022

### California
Williams—Sonoma
576 Sutter Street
San Francisco 94102

# INDEX

**135**